Second-Year Sobriety

Second-Year Sobriety

Getting Comfortable
Now That Everything Is Different

GUY KETTELHACK

HAZELDEN®

INFORMATION & EDUCATIONAL SERVICES

Hazelden
Center City, Minnesota 55012-0176
1–800–328–0094 (Toll-free U.S., Canada, and the Virgin Islands)
1–651–257–1331 (Fax)
www.hazelden.org

Library of Congress Cataloging-in-Publication Data

Kettelhack, Guy.
    Second-year sobriety : getting comfortable now that everything
has changed / Guy Kettelhack.
        p.   cm.
    Originally published: 1st ed. San Francisco : HarperSanFrancisco,
© 1992 (Harper sobriety series ; v. 2).
    Includes bibliographical references.
    ISBN 1–56838–231–6
    1. Alcoholics—Rehabilitation—United States—Case studies.
I. Title.
HV5279.K484   1998
362.292′86—dc21
                                                            98–28453
                                                            CIP

02 01 00 99 98 6 5 4 3 2

Book design by Will H. Powers
Cover design by David Spohn
Typesetting by Stanton Publication Services, Inc.

Contents

V

Author's Note

I'm a recovering alcoholic, and a writer who has grappled for some time with how to express what "recovery" means. The triumph and beauty of recovery from addiction is, to me, endlessly fascinating. Seeking to understand what goes on in recovery seems to me to be exploring what it means to become fully human.

So far, the best way I've found to convey the miraculous consciousness I find in recovery is simply to report what I hear from other recovering people. I've tried to be a kind of journalistic sponge—soaking up information, attempting to pass it on with as little interference as possible. This approach brings me one especially happy dividend: The sponge, as it soaks up information about recovery, ends up profiting as much as anyone else. The adventure of sobriety chronicled in this and other books I've done applies to *me* too. The bottom line is that I feel like a wide-eyed kid listening to what other people tell me about their recovery—as excited and grateful to have been helped by their experience, strength, and hope as I hope you will be too, reading about it in these pages. The spirit of this book can be expressed simply: *We're all in this together.*

What I hope to do here is to offer you, via the voices and insights of hundreds of recovering alcoholics and drug addicts I've listened to across the country, a rich sense of the strange, sometimes frightening, usually baffling, but ultimately wonderful adventure sobriety can mean. Whatever year, month, day, hour, or moment of sobriety you may be facing right now, you will, I hope, find strong evidence herein that you can get through it in full consciousness: You don't have to pick up a drug or a drink. That's the main testament of the people whose stories you'll read here, and the main message of hope. It's our experience that life lived consciously just about always beats life lived blindly. I hope you'll let the people in this book show you how and why, one day at a time, we've found that to be true.

Acknowledgments

Every one of the recovering men and women whose stories are chronicled in this series is owed a debt of gratitude I cannot ever hope to repay, except, perhaps, by passing on their message—that we can all live more fully, joyfully, and consciously, no matter what our "stage" of sobriety—to as wide an audience as possible. I am thankful to them, and to you, for teaching me that we can all live sober and satisfying lives.

Second-Year Sobriety

Introduction

Do the "Terrible Twos" Have to Be Terrible?

On a Saturday morning in September, Keith asked me if we could take a walk through the park so he could talk about something private. We found a good spot out of range of Frisbee throwers and mothers with kids, a bench under a maple tree beginning to blaze red.

Keith was beginning to blaze red too. "I feel like I'm going to explode," he said. "I'm starting to *hate* AA. It's getting to be such a chore going to meetings. I feel like I'm not allowed to be myself in them. As much as everyone always says you can talk about whatever you want to talk about, say anything you want to say, I feel this pressure to be—I don't know—*a good little boy*. The fact is, I think a lot of what I hear in the rooms is a load of crap. Sometimes I want to stand up and tell this or that person to shut up. Like this woman who is constantly complaining about her drunken husband. Why doesn't she just go to Al-Anon? Or that guy who says he's got fifteen years of sobriety who looks and sounds like a basket case. Boy, if that's what sobriety has in store for *me* . . . Or that jerk who runs the morning meeting I go to who gets uptight whenever anyone suggests opening a window, or changing the format of the meeting a little, or . . ."

Keith banged his fists on the bench seat. "The bitch of it is,

3

I can't *tell* anyone how I feel. At least that's what I keep thinking. Aren't I supposed to 'keep the focus on myself'? Not take
anybody's inventory? Certainly not *gossip*. But I gotta tell someone. Sometimes I feel like I've had it up to here with AA. I've
been going for over a year now, and, okay, a lot of stuff is better.
The way I feel physically. The idea of 'showing up for life' really
has helped me. And I get a lot out of the literature. But, damn it,
hearing the same crap over and over again from these jerks I
gotta listen to day after day, what good is any of this doing me?"

Keith's complaints didn't stop here. He went on the express
his fear that Twelve Step programs, and the "sobriety" they pur-
ported to make possible, might just be one more psychological
con game, or worse, as he put it, "a bunch of Moonies." That the
main goal was to turn us all into "jargon-spouting goody two-
shoes." And, he said, whenever he started to talk about any of
these uncomfortable feelings and doubts with most "program
people," they fed him lines. "Keep coming back." "This too shall
pass." Or "Sounds like you need to do the Third [or Fourth or
Eighth or Eleventh] Step."

Keith is talking about a number of classic second-year discomforts, discomforts that lead a lot of people in Twelve Step
programs to label this period in their lives "the Terrible Twos."
But do you have to go through the "Terrible Twos"? Is it some
kind of unavoidable rite of passage?

The research that has produced this book makes it clear that
there are rarely clear divisions between the first and second
years of sobriety: If you've been able to sustain a feeling of well-
being, a sense of joy and adventure, a delight in being sober in
your first year, there's every likelihood you'll continue to feel
those things on even deeper levels in your second year. There's
no need to steel yourself for some kind of unavoidable "Terrible
Twos" territory.

However, Keith's litany of discomforts with Twelve Step

meetings is worth looking at. Judging from the many second-year recoverers who have lent their stories to this book, eruptions of new and very uncomfortable feelings and doubts are by no means uncommon in the second year of sobriety. And the men and women you'll meet here offer some good reasons for this, reasons that are based on a simple, if unnerving, fact. Now that they've spent a year without drugging and drinking, they've spent a year finding out who they really are.

According to Gloria, a woman with fourteen months' sobriety in NA and AA, "There've been a few surprises!" She tabulates some of them: "On the plus side, I now know I *can* get through a year without drinking and drugging. It may sound silly, but I was really scared of the seasons changing. Summer always meant vodka-and-tonic. Fall always meant smoking pot and 'mellowing out.' Winter meant hard liquor: whisky, brandy. Spring meant doing amphetamines." Gloria laughs. "Most people think of the beach, red and golden leaves, Christmas trees, and crocuses when they think of the four seasons. I think of different ways to get blitzed. But the important thing is, now I know I can get through the year *without* getting blitzed. That's a miracle."

Then, says Gloria, there's the "minus" side. "I really thought I'd turn into some sort of perfect person now that I no longer drank or drugged. It was a shock to see that there were whole huge awful areas of my personality that hadn't gone away at all, even after I stopped wrecking my life getting high. This was really depressing. I was still capable of acting out sexually, for example. Or bingeing on food. Or lying to my boss or lover or parents. I was still capable of feeling fear and anxiety and a deep-rooted loneliness that sometimes nothing seems able to touch. Why weren't AA and NA 'fixing' me?"

Echoing Keith, Gloria talks about another surprise: "Sometimes I can't stand going to meetings. It's like a reflex: I zero in on everyone's weakness. I'm full of advice. I feel sometimes like

I know what everyone's problem is, and I can't believe how stupid they all are not to figure out what to do for themselves. Of course, when it comes to my *own* life . . ."

"It's hard to explain," Gloria says after a pause. "But I know that there's some deep dissatisfaction at the center of me that I still haven't reached. I have the idea that this 'void' in the center of me, that deep fear or pain or whatever it is, is the real problem, the real source of why I'm so often impatient and judgmental and anxious back here in my day-to-day life. And I wonder why *that* isn't getting fixed too. I get scared: If AA and NA aren't the answer, what could be? I've tried everything else. . . ."

The Hunger for Comfort in Sobriety

Keith and Gloria are voicing a discomfort common to nearly everyone at some point in their recovery, but perhaps especially in the second year. It's the discomfort of questioning on a deeper level what we're doing, what "recovery" means, what the Twelve Steps and Twelve Step meetings are really all about, what's required of us to keep away from drinking and drugging, and, most important, what it is we really want to do and be in our sober lives. As a man with a little over a year of sobriety says, "Okay, I can stay off booze and drugs. Now what?"

Sometimes there is even a sneaking suspicion that Twelve Step programs are selling us a bill of goods. "They set themselves up as this great alternative to drinking and drugging." Gloria says. "But do they really have the answer to being happy? I mean, aren't they just one more religious-type organization that tries to get you to believe that if you're 'good' you'll get the prize? I can't get away from feeling that sometimes."

It's a feeling that persists even in the face of much eloquent Twelve Step literature that says there is no simple or concrete "prize," that sobriety is an ongoing *process.* "Yeah, yeah, yeah," Keith says in response to this. "I think I'll gag sometimes if I hear the word 'process' again! And all the other stuff too. Like my sponsor saying that all AA is designed to do is to keep me sober. Not get me a lover, find me a job or a new apartment. But is staying sober such a big deal? I mean, okay, I can keep from drinking and drugging. But how do I get *happy?*"

The question of being happy or at least comfortable in sobriety is, on the basis of what so many second-year recoverers have shared with me, clearly an urgent one. The hard truth is that a lot of people in recovery don't make it past their first or second years because they feel sobriety hasn't worked to make them happy. "I'm still not getting what I want," said one woman with thirteen months of sobriety in AA before she picked up another drink. She hasn't come back to AA yet. She may never come back. But from the testimony of those who *do* come back, what she's gone back out to find isn't happiness. It's hell.

Discomfort is very common in the second year of sobriety; becoming acutely aware of our feelings now that we're no longer fleeing them through the escape hatches of drugs or alcohol can be a very uncomfortable process. We're faced with more aspects of ourselves than we're used to seeing, and looking at this whole range of personality is (to put it mildly) rarely an entirely pleasant experience.

The good news is that we don't have to explore this territory unprepared, alone, or by next Tuesday. From the evidence of the recovering people who have shared their experience in this book, it promises to be a lifelong adventure for which we have as much guidance and encouragement as we have the desire or willingness to accept. It's an exploration that also promises to be richly rewarding. The idea that life can be something beyond your wildest dreams seems to become a lot more plausible as you go on.

The portion of this territory that most people seem to travel in their second year of sobriety boils down to a simple idea, expressed in the subtitle of this book: how to get *comfortable* with yourself now that sobriety has turned your old world into something very strange and new.

Achieving Comfort

How to achieve this comfort? Second-year recoverers teach me, first of all, that it's a good idea to take stock of what's gone on in the first year of sobriety. You'll meet a number of men and women who, like Gloria, have delighted in their ability to get through the seasons without responding to some very strong drink or drug signals ("What—Christmas without brandy? The Fourth of July without beer?"), but also to get through other equally provocative situations involving work, love, the supermarket—even serious illness or dealing with death—all without picking up. You deserve to *congratulate yourself* for the extraordinary success you've had in getting from day to day through any number of feelings, crises, and predicaments sober. That's an inescapable miracle.

Second-year recoverers also seem to find themselves facing some difficult questions about recovery and what it means now that they've experienced a year of sobriety. A common question is "Is what I'm going through normal?" You're not alone if you harbor the lingering suspicion that you're *still* a lone duck, still "different" or "less than" (or even "better than"), no matter how much you hear from your sponsor or recovering friends that you're not alone. This worry about being "normal" is usually connected to a tyrannical perfectionism that most second-year recoverers painfully acknowledge in themselves: the frustrating idea that there must be some "ideal" way to be and feel in sobriety that you just haven't been able to achieve yet. This, in turn, can breed some of that judgmentalism that both Keith and Gloria admitted feeling. What do you do about the reflex to "take everybody's inventory," the reflex that makes you tear down anyone you see or hear in or out of Twelve Step meeting rooms? Does it mean you're a "bad" person? That you've failed a test of sobriety? Or does it mean that you just plain *are* superior and you should get the hell out of AA or NA?

And what about the other terrible feelings that don't go away? The anxiety, fear, depression, loneliness, shame, and rage that may continue to afflict you, no matter how assiduously you try to "work your program"? Are you somehow constitutionally incapable of "getting it"? What is "it," anyway? What exactly is sobriety, and what do you have a right to expect from it? Second-year recoverers will share their insights and their paths to greater self-acceptance in these areas, as well as how they're managing to tailor their "programs" to what's comfortable and effective *for them*.

We'll also discover the surprising rewards of reaching out to other people in sobriety, the intriguing things you can learn through what Twelve Step programs call "service": a new, organic sense of Higher Power, of spirituality that seems to grow almost on its own throughout the tumultuous days of your second year; a new way of looking at time, a realization that maybe what's happening to you is happening at exactly the right rate for you, that maybe it's *good* you're not getting what you're convinced you need and want right now; a sense of your life as an ongoing adventure, one with more guidance and more revelation than you ever could have mustered on your own.

One tentative hope that many second-year recoverers have expressed to me is summed up by something Keith finally admitted when he calmed down after his rampage that morning: "The universe may not work the way I think it ought to—but maybe, just maybe, the way it *does* work will turn out to be better than anything I could have thought up on my own. At least," he said, "I'll keep that option open."

one

Taking Stock

Getting through the first year of sobriety means different things to different people. But some of what it means is a matter of simple revelation. You remember when you couldn't imagine getting through summer or winter, a rainy or sunny day, an office party or a family reunion, a Saturday night or a Monday morning without alcohol or chemical "help." Now you've proven to yourself that you can. Physical sobriety may continue to amaze you: Maybe you're still full of gratitude that you're really sleeping now, after so many years of passing out. And there may be any number of other improvements that are as easily quantifiable. Perhaps you're astonished by the responsibilities you've managed to take on and keep up, even if it simply means that you're making it to meetings on a regular basis and calling your sponsor or friends in the program when you say you will.

But there are less easily quantifiable changes, changes that defy easy categorizing. In taking stock of what's gone on in your first year, you'll probably soon find yourself going from external, behavioral changes to inner, emotional ones—new feelings, some of them troubling; new ideas about how the world works (also sometimes troubling); new senses of who you are and what you want to be. It's not easy to articulate this part of the "stock," and yet, on evidence, it is immensely rewarding to try. Because in striving to become conscious of what "sobriety" has meant and continues to mean to you, you're articulating, and thereby getting to know, some important aspects of yourself. "Taking stock" thus becomes a kind of introduction to what you are made of.

It may sound as if we were moving into Fourth Step territory, the Step that asks you to take a "fearless and searching moral inventory" of yourself. If taking an overview of your first year makes you want to go deeper, you may indeed find yourself traveling into the Fourth Step. But the overviews you'll see here aren't meant to be seen as formal Fourth Steps. They're thoughts and impressions from a variety of people who have taken a moment to consider questions like "What exactly happened to me this past year? What did it feel like and what does it feel like now? What have I learned?"

This is rich territory. Sobriety can make life seem like an emotional kaleidoscope, with new feelings, positive and negative, continually forming and re-forming. It's probably impossible (and unnecessary) to keep track of them all, but certain patterns do usually recur; some of the "forms" strike us as more significant than others and are worth noting. They can give us some valuable information about ourselves. We may find, in fact, that we're not so much looking at a kaleidoscope as into a mirror.

This has been Roy's experience. Some of the "stock" he's taken, and that other people in this chapter have taken of their own first year of sobriety, will probably also have some resonance for you.

"I'm Entitled"

"Ever since they wheeled me into the hospital the last time," Roy says with an ironic smile, "I've had the strong clue that I don't have a hell of a lot of power over alcohol and drugs." About fourteen months before, after a desperate day and a half of trying to quit cold turkey on his own, Roy went into severe convulsions from alcoholic withdrawal—"in an AA meeting, of all places," says Roy—and was taken by ambulance to a hospital just in time to save his life.

Roy's life had become clearly "unmanageable" for years before this. By the time of his last drink he was living in a single-room-occupancy welfare hotel in the slums of Detroit; for the past ten years he'd been in and out of hospitals, hospital detox units, and any number of outpatient clinics, none of which had kept him from drinking for longer than a few days at a time. From his vantage point, there had never been a time in his adult life when he wasn't in decline. "Once I was a bright guy everyone thought had potential," Roy says. "Promising kid out of college. Moved to Chicago from a farm town in Kansas in the early sixties. Thought I was gonna be a revolutionary architect—Chicago was the place to be. Instead, I discovered scotch, then pot, then acid, then coke, then scotch again, and then, when I got fired from the last job I was able to get and went on welfare, pints of cheap wine. Chicago, I told myself, was the problem. Big city that ate you alive. So I moved to Detroit. Where things got even worse." Roy developed the growing suspicion that Detroit wasn't the reason they were getting worse. It was not clear to him that he was drinking himself to death.

Now in his second year of recovery, Roy's descent has come to a halt; there's no doubt in this mind about that. "Something about this last time really got to me. Mostly it's that I've got a big, healthy respect for how powerful booze is. I can't get anywhere near the stuff. And my life has gotten better, no doubt about it. Yeah, I'm still living in the same place. I'm still on welfare. I don't have any of the things successful men in their fifties with my education are supposed to have: no car, no house, no family, no bank account. Whoops"—he corrects himself—"I forgot. That's not true anymore! My sponsor helped me open a bank account last week. That's amazing. They even gave me a bank card for the teller machine."

Roy smiles again. "I guess it's this: I've found out that little things count. Being nice to people. Looking after myself better. Washing my clothes. Eating three squares a day. Jeez—what was it we used to say in detox all the time? 'Three hots and a cot.' That's all most guys I knew went into detox for. They certainly didn't give a damn about sobriety. Now I *do* give a damn about sobriety. It's given me all I've got right now, even if what I've got may not look like much."

Roy's face darkens a little. "But it's not all easy, you know. I mean, there are parts of me coming up now that I never knew were there. It's confusing. I can't sort it out, or make it sound logical. There's all this good stuff, how I feel physically, not having diarrhea all the time—all that obvious stuff. I'm amazed that most of the time it doesn't occur to me to drink; for the moment, anyway, that obsession really has been lifted. And for a guy who's been to as many detoxes as me, that's saying something. But—I don't know. I don't miss much now and I'm discovering there was so much that I drank to make *sure* I missed. But now here I am, *all* of me, without that blanket, without that fog of booze all over things. It's not easy. Sometimes I get nuts about this stuff."

What stuff?

Roy looks uneasy. "Well, like sex for example. Booze totally took away my libido by the end. But now that I'm not drinking anymore, it's not only that I'm starting to want to be with a woman—hell, with a lot of women!—but something deeper. I'm lonely. That's the bald truth of it. Sometimes the loneliness feels like it's gonna gut me out. People in AA say they put stuff like sex and taxes, and their mothers and the need to go to the dentist and the rest of it, 'on the shelf.' I'm glad to be told I can do that. But, damn, you can't really put a hunger this strong on the shelf. It blows me away sometimes. I think life has totally passed me by. How am I gonna attract anyone, for one thing? I'm too damned old. And I hardly know what to say to my sponsor, who's a guy, who knows me and cares about me. What would I ever find to say to a woman I just met? It just seems impossible, and it can get so painful I want to . . ." Roy pauses. "Well, I still don't want to drink, thank God. And the thing of it is, even this terrible feeling passes. That old saw 'This too shall pass' turns out to be true. My sponsor tells me, give it time. Talk about it. Don't be afraid to talk about it. But let myself grow a little before I tackle this thing head-on."

The idea that you don't have to be afraid to "talk about it," to really say what you feel, has become the source of another revelation for Roy. "I was so used to people looking at me like I was scum—I mean, I looked and smelled like a bum for the last ten years of my life, so I suppose it shouldn't be a surprise. But I started to believe the expressions in everyone's eyes, that I *was* less than human. This whole thing about low self-esteem: man, mine was deep below the earth's crust, down about magma level. But now—hell, it's the strangest thing. Maybe it's just having gone through a year where I go to meetings and talk to my sponsor and friends in AA, but there's been this strange, slow change in me. People are actually listening to me. They're not looking the other way, or pretending I don't exist, or kicking me. I'll never forget this lady a couple of years ago who poked me aside with her umbrella because I was too near the bus stop she was heading for. Like I was some dog."

Roy's pained look softens. "It's different now. I'm beginning to feel not only that what I have to say might be worth listening to, but that I might actually be able to *depend* on my gut feelings. That I'm actually entitled to have them. I'm entitled to have opinions. I'm entitled to see the world the way I do. It's just as valid as the way anyone else sees the world.

"Whew! It still amazes me sometimes that I can think of myself as having something valid to say! Of course, sometimes I get carried away and go into this self-righteous riff. Funny to think of me slinking around for most of my life, and now I can't keep from judging everybody like I was God or something. Now I know exactly what's wrong with everyone I meet. You can't open your mouth in a meeting before I've sized you up, figured out what you need to do with your life. My sponsor gently suggests that maybe I don't have all the answers. He also says it's pretty normal for all this judgment to be happening right now. I got a lot of opinions bursting to get out! All those years of thinking I wasn't allowed to have any . . ."

But Roy says he generally knows when he's being judgmental. "It's amazing to me just how impatient and pissed off and judgmental I can be," he says. "When I was blitzed, I never felt like that. At least I can't remember feeling it. Basically I lived my life numb. But, you know, that numbness wasn't so bad. I felt sort of complete drunk—like something finally released me. Even that I was *connected* to something. And because I drank with other bums like me, at least I wasn't alone. That feeling of loneliness again—it always comes back to that.

"Sometimes I obsess about all this stuff. How I don't have anything, how old I am, how I'm a big fat failure and there's no hope. I can really do a number on myself. AA then begins to seem like some stupid illusion, like some grown-up version of a kindergarten TV show, full of school marms and little goody two-shoes. Then I go to a meeting, and somebody says something that makes me laugh. And the depression lifts and I'm somewhere else. Somewhere better."

Roy says he sometimes gets so wound up in himself that his mind fills up with a "kind of internal chatter—a buzzing white noise that builds up to a storm. But then, eventually, amazingly, it bursts and fades away." He likens his feelings to "bubbles, one getting big and looking like it's the whole world until it pops, turns into a mist, and is replaced by another. It's confusing, but I guess a big relief, to see so many worlds keep popping and changing into other worlds." Roy groans: "God, I sound like I did in my LSD days." But he knows he's on to something. "You know, I'll be so depressed about what a screw-up I am, then I'll go to a meeting and start laughing, saying stuff in public I never was able to admit to myself even in private, and I'll suddenly see I've changed. That's the lesson again: *things pass.*"

He shakes his head and smiles, bemused. "My sponsor suggests this is how life happens. It's one long, continual change. But underneath that change something more continuous is flowing. A kind of river. Something I can depend on, something that won't go away, and something that has nothing to do with all these bubbles popping up here at the surface. *Something that has nothing to do with my will.* That's the point. My sponsor likes it when I start talking about this, because he knows what a crock I always have thought God and spirituality were. The sixties killed all that stuff for me. But then I go on about this river of continuity down in the center of me, and how sobriety really feels to me like a gift, and *whoa* boy, next thing you know I'm talking about a Higher Power. . . ."

Roy shakes his head again. "All I can say is this. This is somehow the most confused I've ever felt, *and* the most clear. Somehow both at the same time. The stuff I've gone through this past year isn't something I can articulate. Or at least not yet. Most of what I'm talking about now comes to me as a kind of glimmer— something vague on the horizon. But it's there. And I keep having the feeling that whatever it is, I'm getting closer to it."

"My Puppet Emotions, My Puppet Life . . ."

Margery, like Roy, is struck by how deep and painful the loneliness has been in her first year of sobriety. Unlike Roy, she was able even through the last years of her drinking to continue having relationships, even to continue working as the head of a day care center. "Nobody at work knew I had a drinking problem," she says. "Or at least, if they did they weren't letting on. I only drank at night. But I made up then for what I didn't drink during the days." Margery said she went to bed with a bottle of brandy ("I'd wake up a dozen times a night and take a swig out of it") when she couldn't go to bed with a man. "And even when I did go to bed with a man," she says, "I made sure we didn't go to bed without a heavy alcoholic 'aphrodisiac.'" Married and divorced three times, each time to an alcoholic, and with any number of "casual" lovers, as often as not pick-ups at her local bar, Margery had had, for most of her life, a very active love life. "Actually, I don't know how much 'love' entered into it," she says. "But whatever was going on with all those guys, it was active."

Margery decided to quit drinking, she says, "in stages. It first occurred to me that I wasn't happy with my life when I found this pamphlet put out by the Hemlock Society and spent the next few days fantasizing about how I might kill myself. I hadn't been with a man I'd really liked, much less loved, in years. I felt like an automaton at work. I was as caring and sweet and professional and motherly as I knew how to be with all my little charges at the day care center, but inside I was dead already. Killing myself would just have been killing the rest of me: the outer part, the puppet part that was going through the motions."

Margery had heard of AA; one of her ex-husbands had been "in and out of the rooms" for years in the same New England city she still lived in, so she even knew where meetings were held. "I decided to walk into one, sit at the back of the room. Some big ex-con was talking about passing out in a subway tunnel and getting awakened by a rat nibbling at his toes." Margery says she "couldn't relate—to tell the truth, I went running out of the room," and went back to drinking. But she tried another meeting some weeks later and felt a little more receptive: "I thought it was very nice what all those people were doing for themselves." She gradually came to feel that she might be "one of them."

Margery says she didn't have a dramatic bottom: "I just felt I'd had it. Had it up to here with the emptiness I felt inside me. I knew it was time for something to happen, to let something in." She hasn't had a drink in over a year, and much of the physical and emotional improvements we've heard Roy talk about apply to her too. "Sobriety has brought me a lot of wonderful changes," Margery says. "But it's brought other things too. Awarenesses, mainly. Or rather, the awareness that I'm *not* aware."

She attempts to explain. "No one is more accommodating or works harder than I do," she says. "I've got incredible drive. I mean, I ran this day care center—and it's one of the best in the state—all while I was drinking and screwing around with strange men nearly every night. I've always known there's something in me that's desperate to succeed. And now that I'm not strung out every day from late nights of booze and sex, I seem to be doing an even better job. I'm just mentally *present* in a way I wasn't before, when I was hung over every day. But I'm sort of emotionally *absent* too. . . ."

Margery says that when she heard a few weeks before that her last ex-husband had died of a heart attack, she was appalled at her response. Although he was the only one of her three husbands that she feels she really loved, she says, "I felt nothing. It was strange. I kept wondering, Why aren't you crying? Why don't you miss him? We'd been friends, talked to each other on the phone all the time. He was even a kind of confidant to me. But I couldn't muster up any response, except a vague feeling that it was 'too bad.' I couldn't even hate myself for not feeling anything! It was like I'd gone all dead inside."

Margery shrugs. "But now I'm starting to think, Is it any wonder I feel emotionally numb? I've been pouring so much energy into being accommodating and 'successful'—good and right and the best—it's like this constant effort is draining something from my core. . . . I find I can't feel much of anything. This is a little distressing, although I have to say I feel so distanced from everything I don't get too upset about it. But, vaguely, I find myself wondering, Is my life a complete sham? All the 'caring' things I do for others, is it all some dumb show? I mean, caring—caring for little children all day long—is my business. And you should see the letters I get from parents. How much their kids look forward to coming here. How they wish they could be as good with kids as I am. I've got a wonderful reputation for being sweet and understanding and reliable. I'd risk my life to save a kitten, that's how I've always thought of myself, and how other people have always seen me. But the truth is, something in the center of me isn't touched. Not at all. Not by anything."

Margery stops for a moment; her tone becomes more sharply pained. "Who am I kidding? Not feel anything?" She manages a bitter smile. "The loneliness. That sometimes knocks me silly, how lonely I can get. . . .

"I'm no longer going to bed with just anyone," she says, "which quite frankly has caused some huge withdrawal pains. Sex to me was so linked with alcohol that I don't dare, at least for now, to jeopardize myself by getting back into the sexual pattern I was in before. But I can't tell you how angry I get when I pass a man I find attractive and there's no response back from him." Margery laughs a little. "It's as if I think it's a man's *duty* to be attracted to me! The feeling is, how dare the world not be hungry for me when I'm so hungry for the world!" Margery looks up, struck by this last thought. "I guess I'm not so numb after all. This overwhelming loneliness, and hunger. Hunger is a feeling, isn't it? A very strong feeling, in my case . . ."

Drinking, Margery says, provided a great wash over that hunger, as well as all her other feelings. "Drinking allowed me to play all sorts of roles. Femme fatale. Entertainer. Witty compatriot of brilliant people. Which brings up another thing. I was never really confident about my own intelligence and talents, so I was a goner for any guy who seemed special. I was magnetized by 'geniuses.' In fact, I devoted my life to finding them and making them love me—or if they couldn't do that, at least find me indispensable. That's the story of each of my three marriages: one was a sullen alcoholic painter, another a moody alcoholic classical violinist, the last one a brooding alcoholic poet." Margery sighs with exhaustion. "God, the grasping and the trying and the controlling—pushing them to reach heights, typing poems, cleaning up paint, calling their agents . . . and then being the perfect 'mother' of three dozen children during the day. It just squeezed me dry. Alcohol allowed me to keep up the ruse, but then that solution became the problem: As I got more drunk and more desperate, I couldn't attract who I wanted to attract. In the end, alcohol started to keep me from meeting my 'genius' men. So now that my whole former life is gone—the booze and the men—I'm left with . . . what?"

Margery looks down at her hands, which are clenched together in her lap. "It's like there's something vestigial inside me, deep beneath the numb outer layers. A kind of clutching hand in the center of me with a life of its own, a kind of insensate baby whose only impulse is to grab, grab, grab. Who I might be as a grown, forty-three-year-old woman, I don't know. Who I might have become in all these years of desperate hunger and grasping, I don't have a clue. And so now when I'm called upon to 'feel'— now that I don't have the help of alcohol (and alcohol was a kind of acting teacher to me, enabling me to convey every 'appropriate' emotion in the book)—I just can't come up with the goods. It's been so long since I've been in touch with the feeling part of me, the part of me that maybe really is me, that I'm at a complete loss. If I'm honest, all I can ever make myself aware of is that grasping blind baby in my heart." Margery laughs feebly. "No wonder I hate all that John Bradshaw stuff about the 'inner child.' I'm terrified of admitting that I've got one inside of me! Oh, it's not that I can't keep the ruse up. Even, in my way, care about things. I mean, I've got a cat, and I love him. But that kind of love is sort of blissing-out, which, come to think of it, I also try to do in meditation. Meditation and my cat—what I really want them to do is make me escape my pain the way alcohol used to do so reliably."

Margery is amazed she's let this much out about how she feels. "I don't usually speculate so much about why I feel the way I do. I don't really trust analysis; it doesn't get me anywhere. But maybe this isn't analysis, or at least not some detached, abstract kind. Maybe all I'm doing is trying to say how I feel." She looks a little dismayed that this could be happening. Then she smiles. "If I'm honest, it's not all so bleak. One of the things I feel is hope. That the blind insensate baby inside me will one day gain sight and ears and senses and limbs and begin to apprehend the world on her own. That I'll one day shed my puppet emotions, my puppet life, and start to see what *Margery* is all about. What *she* really might want to be and do in her life."

Margery says she is sure of one thing. Her tentative movement toward hope wouldn't—couldn't—be happening if she were still drinking. "The door to a new life may still have only opened a crack, even after more than a year of sobriety, but at least it's open. I can't tell you how tightly locked it was before. . . ."

Margery and Roy describe many of the warning feelings common to second-year recoverers. What seems clear in each of their experiences, and in those of so many others in their second year, is that life isn't a movie. Feelings don't happen on cue. They seem to come from what sometimes seems an impossibly mysterious source. As often as not, they surprise the hell out of us. It's as if our outer shell begins to crack, like the earth's crust in an earthquake, allowing any amount of inner, unanticipated emotional "stuff" to seep up or erupt at the surface.

While you didn't consciously make the decision to start *feeling* when you decided to stop drinking and drugging, that seems to be the inescapable dividend. Now that you're sober, you're becoming conscious of a whole new and unexplored world, not only the "out there" world of work and family and friends, but the world within yourself.

Loneliness

It's not surprising that loneliness is such a pervasive product of this newly discovered "inner world." So many people in their second year of sobriety talk about feeling naked, alone, defenseless, and inadequate. Feeling unprotected by the old buffers of alcohol and drugs, we often feel we're working without a net. (The fact that we've spent a year *successfully* working without a net doesn't always make us feel all that secure; sometimes we just feel lucky.) Our perceived imperfections, contradictory emotions, mood swings, "dark" selves—all of this can make us feel terribly isolated and, what's especially painful, undeserving of the kind of loving attention we're offered every day by people in Twelve Step programs.

For this reason, it can be excruciating for some people to even open their mouths in a Twelve Step meeting. "I spend almost all the meeting rehearsing what I'm going to say when it's my turn to speak," says Jack, a man with fifteen months of sobriety. "It's so important to me that I sound good. It's like a performance—I'm revving up for the big finale," Jack sighs exhaustedly. "Of course, while I'm preparing my speech, I can't hear anything anybody's saying. That's why I try to get called on first: so that I can get my stuff out and start to listen to what other people have to say!" Marilyn, with just over a year of sobriety, says, "I try to say, 'My name is Marilyn and I'm an alcoholic,' in every meeting I go to, just to practice talking in a group. Speaking in front of so many people terrifies me; I still can't imagine saying more than that. Everyone else sounds like they took public speaking lessons. Where does everyone learn to talk so openly and smoothly? I feel like such an idiot when I try to put my feelings into words. . . ."

Marilyn and Jack, along with Margery and Roy, admit to frequent periods of feeling deeply lonely as they go through the process of fitting themselves into the world they find around them now that they're sober. So do many other recovering people. We all go through periods of feeling confused and lonely, and never more than in the second year of sobriety. But these painful feelings do seem to lessen as we allow ourselves to practice *acknowledging* what we feel to ourselves and to somebody else, especially the "somebody else" of a meeting.

Adjusting to sobriety, with its difficult emotional times, isn't the only reason we may feel alone or lonely. Each of us is psychologically unique, and we may each have any number of historical reasons for feeling more hobbled than the next person by the prospect of any kind of relationship or social encounter. And with its cutthroat emphasis on competition, getting ahead, and looking out for Number One, our culture can breed apartness. No wonder loneliness is endemic, not only among recovering alcoholics and addicts but in the population generally.

Recovering alcoholics and addicts do seem to have an edge in getting over this loneliness, or at least facing it without drugs or booze. We learn that even the most debilitating feelings of loneliness pass. Loneliness turns out to be a feeling, and like every other feeling, it's not permanent. I have never met a recovering person who's completed a year of sobriety without having some version of this realization: "I can get through it without picking up. Even the worst stuff passes. None of what I thought would kill me does kill me." Not even loneliness.

As recovering people also teach me, when we're faced with feelings of loneliness we can learn to do other things besides waiting for them to pass. A good beginning for most people is to pick up the phone, or simply go to a Twelve Step meeting. We learn there are always people with whom we can make contact. But it helps to know that the extra-painful stab we sometimes feel, the pit-of-the-stomach loneliness that can seem to overwhelm us, has a built-in obsolescence; we can learn to find some reassurance in the certainty that it will pass.

Allowing yourself to accept the arrival and passage of even the most disturbing and contradictory feelings does seem to be a matter of practice—and patience. Look at Abigail's experience with "stock taking" at the end of her first year for a clue to what this can mean in some more specific ways.

"Allowing Myself to Be One and a Half"

"About three months after my first-year anniversary in AA," Abigail says, "my sister and her husband, who live a sort of back-to-nature life in a log cabin near a small town in northern New England, invited me to stay for a few days." Her sister and brother-in-law had a baby, eighteen months old, whom she had never seen before. "I always felt tense and competitive with my sister," Abigail explains, "and I felt especially jealous of the fact that she had a happy marriage and now a baby. When I still drank, I had terrible resentments about her. Sort of mom-always-liked-you-best. Which, as it happens, was true. My mother was always comparing us and finding me wanting. So I kept my distance from my sister, even after I first got sober. I called her up to congratulate her when Clarissa was born—but, well, I guess I was still jealous. I wanted a family too. But all I seemed capable of was being an alcoholic."

After a year of sobriety, and with a stronger sense of self-esteem, Abigail says, "I could feel some real gratitude and pride about being a *recovering* alcoholic." She decided to say yes to her sister's invitation. "I felt I could see my sister without hating her or myself. I was up-front about the fact that I needed to go to AA meetings, and there were meetings in a nearby town, so that was taken care of."

However, Abigail's main sense of curiosity and anxiety centered less on seeing her sister again than it did on meeting the baby. "I was so curious about Clarissa. After all, she was my niece. I wondered, would she look like me? Would she like me?

It confused me, how anxious I was . . ." Abigail pauses. "I imagined all sorts of terrible scenarios. What if Clarissa went into a screaming fit the moment she saw me? *That* would be like someone in my family," she laughs. "I had no real idea why I was so scared to meet this little baby, but I was."

It turned out Abigail didn't have to worry about Clarissa not liking her. Her eyes open wide at the memory. "When I got there and saw this strawberry blonde baby girl sitting in the midst of her toys and picture books, I was dumbstruck. Suddenly and completely enchanted." It seems Clarissa was too. "I've never had a reaction like that from anyone before, male or female, old or young. Clarissa took one look at me, waddled up, and reached out, beaming, to be picked up. You know," Abigail smiles warmly as she continues, "I never knew 'beaming' could be such a literal truth. It's like *light* came out of that little girl. I had the funny feeling we'd known each other in a dozen past lives. Almost like the only point of me being my sister's sister was to be around so that I could meet Clarissa!"

Abigail and Clarissa were inseparable for most of the weekend, "My sister was amused at first, then maybe a little jealous. I mean, apparently Clarissa had never reacted like this to anyone before, not even her parents! We spent hours with her books. She loves picture books about animals; I'm convinced she's going to grow up to be a veterinarian. We made animal sounds at each other with the greatest care and seriousness. She had 'moooo' down pat, but 'quack' was a little beyond her. I know it sounds weird, but I've never had such fun with anybody, ever. She was sister, daughter, friend—everything."

But she was also a kind of teacher. "Eighteen months is a funny time," Abigail says. "You're able to walk and you can talk a little and you're big enough to start exploring the world. If you're in a loving environment, you bring a natural sense of wonder to everything you see and touch. But it's not all easy. Like one time Clarissa sat in her high chair at mealtime demanding food.

We had a big salad, full of greens and things my sister had grown herself in a big summer vegetable garden in the backyard. Clarissa loved the little cherry tomatoes in the salad, and because I was her ally, she knew she could get as many as she wanted from me. She called them 'tommy.' She was like a little queen. She looked at me, said 'tommy,' and expected quite naturally that I would reach into the salad bowl and give her one. And of course I did—then two, then three—up to six. But my sister said Clarissa would get sick if she ate too many 'tommies.' So, by the seventh demand, I had to say no."

Clarissa did not take very well to "no." "At first she looked at me with deep shock. Then, as if bestowing regal forgiveness, she smiled politely and repeated, 'tommy.' When I shook my head and said no, trying to keep her good favor by goo-gooing, mooing, and quacking at her, she began to lose patience. Actually, she looked at me as if I were a little soft in the head. '*Tom-mee,*' she repeated, with emphasis, as if attempting to communicate with someone particularly dimwitted." Abigail laughs a little nervously, reliving the moment. "It was terrible. I couldn't stand saying no to Clarissa. I pleaded—actually pleaded!—with my sister, could she have just one more? But no, my sister said she couldn't, and spoke sharply to Clarissa who busied herself with emptying the lettuce leaves and macaroni and cheese on her plate onto the floor." Worse, Abigail says, "Clarissa avoided looking at me. I'd let her down so terribly."

Used to the messes caused by Clarissa, Abigail's sister and brother-in-law got up from their chairs, got out the mop, and routinely set about cleaning up the food on the floor. As they were mopping up, Clarissa addressed Abigail again. "'Down,'" Abigail says Clarissa quietly instructed her—"again like this little royal person. My sister said it was okay, Clarissa could get down if she wanted to, so I reached over, pulled her out of her high chair, and put her on the floor. She didn't cry; she just ran away into the living room. I felt devastated. After feeling this incredible bond to this little baby girl, I couldn't stand her rejection."

Terribly upset, Abigail joined Clarissa in the living room, not sure what to do. Luckily, owing to the happy phenomenon of an eighteen-month-old's short attention span, "everything was okay. She mooed at me and laughed and we were on the floor again, being cows and ducks and horses and dogs. I was so relieved. But I was also intrigued. Because, later, when I had time to think about the day—doing my 'Tenth Step,' as I would have told my sponsor!—I saw that I'd learned something very interesting. Not just about Clarissa but about myself."

Abigail realized that she saw *herself* in Clarissa. "If anything," she says, "Clarissa was ahead of me. In sobriety, anyway, I hadn't made it to the eighteen-month mark yet! And I had to admit, all of the wonder and curiosity, as well as the devastation at hearing the word *no*—all of that was exactly what I felt, sober. Clarissa's moods and emotions were like giant primary-color cut-outs: everything was larger than life, more wonderful than could be believed, more terrible than could be imagined. I realized that I felt the same way. But more than that, I needed to give myself *permission* to feel that way."

Abigail realized in this moment that it was okay to feel as raw and dumbstruck and full of emotion as an eighteen-month-old baby, which, in some sense, was exactly how she felt. "Of course, I'm not always pleased about this," Abigail says. "I mean, I also have to play the responsible adult. Go to work. Do my laundry. Be where I say I'll be. 'Show up for life,' as they say in AA. Sometimes I wish I could go the whole way and sit up there next to Clarissa in a high chair dumping my macaroni and cheese on the floor. But I can't do that. And so—and I guess this is a big part of my revelation—I've felt a little ashamed. I mean, if I'm supposed to be an adult, why can't I just do what my mother and father keep hoping I'll do? Get my act together? Create a life like my sister's? There's this awful tension, somehow, between all this sober adult responsibility I'm supposed to keep up in my outer life and the emotional baby I still am inside. I don't know how to reconcile the two, so sometimes I just try to hide the baby, pretend I'm more mature and sober than I am. But that never works. Because I know who I am inside. . . . "

Something about seeing Clarissa freed Abigail to accept her emotional "babyhood" without judging it. "I've been so afraid to make decisions of any kind," Abigail says, "I guess because I always knew there was this baby inside me who didn't know how to make decisions. Who in her right mind would entrust important decisions to a baby?" But Abigail is taking a different tack on this now. "How does a one-and-a-half-year-old get to be two? Or a two-year-old get to be three? How do you get from one stage to another to another and grow up? By making mistakes, usually. By *doing it anyway.* Sometimes you fall down. Sometimes you get bruised. But you keep learning. You keep going on. I'm not sure why seeing Clarissa made all this clear to me—maybe simply because she helped me to identify my own 'baby' nature and accept it. But I also see that the point isn't to stay a baby. It's to grow up. And somehow I'm ready now to take a few more risks. I'm getting at least a tiny bit more comfortable with the idea that I don't have to do this sobriety thing perfectly. Or live life perfectly. And, maybe most important, that my outsized feelings won't kill me as I go about this crazy process of getting better. Of recovering."

Toward a Healing Acceptance

Abigail admits that she may sound more "together" about this process than she feels. "I can't always be this sweetly reasonable about myself," she says. "There are times when I do just throw the macaroni on the floor, and I don't always clean it up right away, either." Those "outsize emotions" she can't help having do sometimes wreak havoc. But the answer for her, and for others who have taken stock of where they are and what they're feeling after a year or more of sobriety, seems to lie ultimately in a kind of *permission* to experience feelings, a full acceptance of wherever it is we happen to be.

This acceptance can turn out to be amazingly healing. As one man with eighteen months of sobriety put it, "It really amounts to working the First Step all over again. Surrendering to my powerlessness over who I am right at the moment. I can't pretend to have insights I don't have." He echoes Abigail in this, when she said she used to try to "hide the baby . . . pretend I'm more sober and mature than I am." A terrible price is paid when we hide who we are, a price we remember from our drinking or drugging days, when most of us spent nearly all our waking hours hiding who we were. It's just as painful to hide in sobriety as it is to hide when you're an active addict or alcoholic. Or maybe, as a second-year recovering friend suggests, it's *more* painful to hide sober than when you're drunk or high. We're simply more conscious of the pain of hiding now.

This slow emergence of self, based on an acceptance of who you are *right now*, is rarely accomplished smoothly. As Abigail puts it, "Sometimes you fall down. Sometimes you get bruised. But you keep learning. You keep going on." In the process of "going on," we can't seem to help colliding with new and sometimes seemingly insurmountable obstacles. It's the experience of the people in this book that you can tap into an abundant source of help to deal with these collisions. The payoff can be an extraordinary new sober self, one with surprising strength and resilience. But whatever new you begins to emerge, it's almost always a surprise. You can go through long periods of doubting that what's happening to you is "normal." You can be convinced, in the thick of struggling with any number of "demons" that seem to attack you in sobriety, that you're alone again. That there's really no help to be had.

But there is help to be had. And what may seem to be terribly abnormal as you go about seeking that help can sometimes turn out to be very normal indeed. What is normal in sobriety—particularly as it seems to be experienced in the second year? That's what we'll consider next.

two

Discovering What's Normal—For You

Margery admitted feeling a kind of distance, not only from other people but from her own feelings. You, too, may have become so used to numbing yourself to your feelings and the consequences of your actions that you now need to remind yourself regularly of some pretty basic realities. As one woman with sixteen months in NA put it, "Yes, I am a human being, I do exist, what I feel does count, and what affects other people affects me as well. It's finally beginning to register that the law of gravity just might apply to *me* too."

Resistance may linger to the idea that you're the same brand of human as other people. Sometimes you're not quite convinced that who they're talking about in NA or AA is *you*. It's what might be called the "Yeah, but . . ." syndrome. You hear something you "sort of" identify with, then instantly think something like, "Yeah, but you're still not me. You still haven't had the background I've had. You aren't facing exactly what I'm facing. You're not [choose one:] a struggling single mother; HIV-positive; a fifty-year-old bachelor; a CEO in a major company; Hispanic or Black or Irish or Polish or Italian; as young (or as old) as I am; living with your mother; physically disabled; manic-depressive; gay; straight; Buddhist or Catholic or Jewish. . . ."

There is no end to the number of categories you may feel separate you from others.

As much as we hear the motto "Identify, don't compare" in Twelve Step meetings, it can be very hard not to compare—which makes it easy to continue to feel isolated and unique. Convinced that we're not, after all, like anyone else, we can easily slip into telling ourselves that what works for other people couldn't possibly work for us. We are simply too far from some imagined norm to be reached. We are doomed to aloneness. This is a dangerous state: It doesn't take a huge leap to go from this feeling back to a drink or a drug. (Poor me, poor me, pour me a drink. . . .)

Feeling alone or isolated is a natural, temporary product of the seemingly inevitable confusions and fears we experience as we adjust to day-to-day sober life. It's normal to *wonder* if you're normal when you experience life as a sober person. *Can* you really ever get better, lose the desire to get blitzed, lose the desire to check out of life? Do you feel grateful to be recovering? Should you? When people around you talk about serenity, or what it feels like to "surrender," "turn it over," or rely on a "Higher Power," do you really know what they're talking about? Is your particular brand of recovery the *right* brand? Are you where you should be?

Or, as is a common sneaking suspicion, is it all a lot of hogwash? Are you just deluding yourself that, someday, you might actually know satisfaction in your life? Are you ever going to get what you need, feel true self-acceptance and a sense of inner peace, understand what it means to experience the "promises" that you hear so much about in Twelve Step meetings?

I have yet to meet a recovering person who felt "normal" as he or she entered sobriety. Indeed, it seems that most of us became willing to get sober precisely because something in the center of us felt so *abnormal*, so terribly out-of-whack. So much of second-year sobriety seems to be bound up in the slow, awkward discovery, and then acceptance, of what's "normal," or right, *for each of us.* We learn that no one can make this discovery for us; we have to make it for ourselves.

Sadly, not everybody does.

A Fatal Assumption: "I Can't Be Reached"

The primary mission of this book is to celebrate the triumph of people in their second year of sobriety who develop a sense of connectedness, a feeling that what they're doing is sufficient, normal (for them), nurturing, life-enhancing—sober.

Kevin was not able to forge this connection. He wasn't able to survive his own fears, his self-mistrust, the conviction that he was abnormal and beyond any real help. While much remains unclear about Kevin's motivations, one thing is clear: He made a bedrock assumption that he couldn't be "reached."

Kevin and I got sober at about the same time. We both went to the same early-morning meeting, and, while we never exchanged phone numbers or became more than acquaintances, I felt a bond of sympathy with him when he spoke and during the occasional conversation we had before or after a meeting.

I was lucky: I was an alcoholic desperate for help, and I managed to get that help. So far, I haven't turned away from the source of it. Through some kind of spiritual gift, shared by a good many other recovering addicts and alcoholics, I've somehow managed to enjoy my sobriety without a break.

Kevin was not so lucky. He had a painful history of "going back out" before I knew him: acquiring a month, then maybe two months, once as long as eleven months of sobriety, then, as he put it, "giving up." "It's no use," his friends told me he used to say. "Sobriety is for other people."

When he returned to AA the last time, Kevin still wasn't talking about his fears and doubts. He gave the impression he didn't need to. His favorite slogan about sobriety was "You have to give it away to keep it." And give he did. He was unfailingly helpful to and interested in other people. He was available to anyone who had practical problems—the first to help you paint your kitchen, move your furniture, take care of your cats when you were away. He was quiet about it; in fact, he went to great pains not to let people know how much help he gave. But word got around anyway. You could always depend on Kevin. No one listened better than Kevin did. No one would come through for you more than he. But he never said what was in his own heart. On the rare occasions he spoke about his life, he became nearly monosyllabic. "You know, sometimes I get depressed," he'd say. "But it's all right. I'm okay." It was a Kevinism to say, "I pass— I'll just listen today," at our round-robin morning meeting. He even became a kind of power of example in this regard. People who felt they ran on at the mouth at meetings would declare they wished they were more like Kevin. At peace. Serene. Somebody who didn't need to dominate a meeting. Someone who was content to listen.

Then, at one morning meeting, Kevin finally did share something personal. He'd made it to the eighteen-month mark, something he'd never done before. He said he wanted the group to know this, but he seemed curiously detached. There was no real look of pride or even happiness in his eyes. This may have been due to something else he'd decided to divulge that morning. While cleaning his closet, he said, he discovered an unopened quart of vodka. He didn't drink it, he said; he didn't even want to drink it. But he thought he'd leave it there anyway. Just as a reminder of the fact that he didn't want to drink. As a kind of "monument," in his word, to what would happen to him if he ever picked up a drink again.

Although what he said took up less than a minute of meeting time, Kevin had never talked openly or volubly about himself before. The rest of us were worried. Many people shared that they didn't think keeping that kind of temptation in the house was a good idea. After the meeting, a number of people separately suggested to Kevin that he get rid of the bottle. It had been their experience that any alcoholic who kept alcohol in the house was courting disaster. But Kevin just nodded impassively. He wasn't going to do anything about it just yet.

The next day Kevin wasn't at the meeting. Nor the day after that. We finally learned, three days later, that Kevin had drunk the vodka. Then he had hanged himself.

"I'm just different from you," Kevin used to tell his recovering friends. He once privately admitted that he never felt anyone could possibly understand him or help him. He felt he was and always would be "the odd man out."

There is no simple moral to Kevin's story. No one's life can be reduced to a cautionary tale. There was, undoubtedly, much going on inside him that nobody knew about. It is entirely possible that he suffered from clinical depression in addition to his alcoholism; he might have benefited from professional help, a kind of help Twelve Step programs were never meant or equipped to provide. But while Kevin is no simple example of anything, he does give us the painful reminder that we cannot receive even the hope of help until we truly ask for it—*cry out for it*, if we have to.

A friend of Kevin's, also working on his second year of sobriety, said he was very shaken by what happened because he could see how close he had been to feeling equally unreachable. "But then, by the grace of what I call 'God,'" he said, "I somehow realized I didn't have to starve for help. I had the choice to accept it. In fact, it was all around me. I pray I'll never forget I always have access to that abundance."

Toward a New View of What's "Normal"

The abundance that recovering people speak of, and that we sometimes understand is infinitely available to us, can at other times seem like wishful thinking. And losing that sense of abundance can have tragic consequences. But even if it doesn't lead to tragedy, it can still lead to pain—pain that may threaten to become unbearable. Few recovering people don't experience periodic losses or diminution of hope. It can be hard to trust that what we hear again and again in "the rooms" is true: that we'll be taken care of. It may not seem possible to think that all we have to do is ask for guidance, and trust that we have all the resources we need to take the next right step in our lives.

In the quest for this guidance and receptivity, some of us cling with a vengeance to the Serenity Prayer:

God grant me the serenity to accept the things I cannot change
The courage to change the things I can
And the wisdom to know the difference

Sharon, a schoolteacher with fourteen months of sobriety, says she certainly does, but that this attitude of vengeance doesn't always serve her. "I love the Serenity Prayer," she says. "It's probably the greatest capsule of wisdom I've ever come across. But, to tell the truth, I don't really ever think of it until my back's against the wall. Then I recite it to myself frantically, usually getting the words all mixed up! And at these times, it doesn't always seem to calm me down or help me. My sponsor says the problem might be that when I only use the Serenity Prayer at extreme times, I'm so anxious that I forget the prayer is a *request*. That I'm *asking* for all this stuff—this serenity, courage, and wisdom—to be *granted* to me."

Like Sharon, many other second-year recoverers tell me that they experience similar moments of knotting up inside. They feel unable even to imagine getting help. They forget how to be receptive to the possibility of guidance. Like so many of the rest of us, in the grip of such feelings as boredom, resentment, impatience, or self-mistrust, they clench. Then when they look frantically for answers, the very desperation of the search can get in the way. It's as if they were trying to squeeze an answer out of the world (or out of the phone on which they call their recovering friends and sponsors). Unfortunately, it's the experience of most recovering people that the world almost never yields to this kind of frontal assault.

When we're in this frantic state, the Serenity Prayer can seem pretty inadequate, because we've forgotten a crucial aspect of it, or of any prayer: its implicit cry for help, for guidance from *something outside our own power.* Instead, we rail at our inability to give serenity, courage, or wisdom to *ourselves*—beating ourselves up for something we're sure, out of inadequacy, we're doing wrong. Sharon says, "I often feel that if I were only a better person, I'd *get* some of what the Serenity Prayer promises. I convince myself it's a failure of my own will when I don't." In the state of self-absorption and self-hate this can engender, it seems obvious that you just don't have the "stuff." A secret suspicion you may long have harbored is confirmed: The rewards of sobriety are for other people, not for you.

Even more galling, you look around to see other recovering people who don't seem to be as tormented by life as you are. Sometimes, in fact, it seems everyone is less tormented, and so much better than you are at managing life. This drives in another wedge, and more suspicions are confirmed. You may decide you're just not "normal" or reachable the way the rest of these recovering people seem to be. You're alone, and you always will be.

If there's one overriding classic second-year dilemma, it's this nagging feeling of *separateness.* How do you deal with it? How do you find a path in recovery that makes sense to you, that works for you, that gives you the prospect and experience of greater serenity and self-acceptance? That makes you feel a part of the world, not apart from it?

We'll meet some people now who might give us a clue. People who, in their second year, have been able to face some devastating feelings; that they were beyond help, that they weren't "normal," that sobriety was for everybody but them. Then we'll see how they've learned to keep from splitting away from their recovery resources, even at the worst moments of an emotional siege. We'll see them face and eventually get beyond the debilitating feelings we've referred to before, feelings very few second-year recoverers manage to avoid: boredom, resentment, impatience, and self-hate. Leroy, Rebecca, and Jeffrey are all smack in the middle of their second year of sobriety. The passages they're making have meaning for anyone struggling toward sober selfhood, but especially for second-year recoverers.

"Will I Ever Have a Good Time Again?": ### Leroy

Leroy, in Milwaukee, sometimes thinks he'll die of loneliness and boredom in AA and NA. Sick of program jargon, feeling as if he just doesn't know how to talk to or be with people now that he's not getting high, he wonders: "Will I ever have a good time again?"

"I feel like some part of me hasn't quite caught up to the rest of me," Leroy explains. "My body is sober. I feel better, a lot of my health problems disappeared. I don't have high blood pressure anymore—drinking turned out to be the major cause of that. But as great as all the physical improvement is, you do get used to it after a while. It's hard to keep cranking up the old gratitude. Especially when nothing else in my life is much fun. I mean, after fifteen months of sobriety, how excited can you get that you don't have hangovers anymore?"

Leroy says that his job as a salesman for a pharmaceutical company has become stifling. "I never realized how much alcohol helped to lubricate my lunches and the sales pitches that I gave at them. Now I look at some guy across from me drinking martinis and I can't think of anything to say. All my sales talk sounds stupid. All I want to do is get out of there." Leroy feels that his first fifteen months of sobriety have also had a detrimental effect on his ability to shine at business meetings, especially the local Black Businessmen's Council, of which he'd always been a very vocal and energetic member. "I'm not taking the crazy risks I took before, which I know sounds like it's a healthy change, but there are some guys I work for, or on the council, who are wondering what happened to the old 'spark.' I'm not promising to deliver the world anymore. Truth is, I just don't *care* as much as I used to. And I can't lie about it. And I don't care about exceeding sales records, giving my life over to the glory of my company, becoming a shining example of a successful black businessman, and all that other stuff."

It would help, Leroy says, if his life outside the office were any better than it is in the office, but so far it's been disappointing. "It was great to realize in AA that there were other people out there who were recovering from alcoholism," he says, "but I freeze before and after meetings. I usually love what people talk about, I share about my own stuff, but when there's even the prospect of a one-on-one, I don't know what to say or do. I can't seem to develop friendships outside the rooms. I can't even really hold on to a sponsor. Technically, I've got one because they told me to get one, but I was careful to choose a real non-intervention-type guy, which means I almost never talk to him, and he's never once picked up the phone to see how I was."

So what does Leroy do after work? "Not much. TV's a pretty lame pastime. I used to get sloshed and watch these nature shows on the public television station; you know, all those snakes swallowing rodents, and lions eating zebras, and monkeys picking fleas off each other. I said to myself, hmm, this looks okay, and then drank myself into oblivion. But none of that has much interest for me now. And the rest of the time, the time I used to spend in bars, I guess that's what I miss the most. Even if I had no real friends, at least I had the illusion of a party going on all the time. That's what was so great about bars. For the price of a night's worth of drinking, you got a party. But now—*damn*, sometimes I think if I see another cup of coffee or herb tea or whatever the hell else I'm supposed to drink at night instead of booze, I'll go nuts. And a coffee shop is not a substitute for a bar, God knows."

What about working the program? Doesn't he get some help or solace from that?

"When I'm actually in a meeting," Leroy says, "when people are really being honest about their feelings, sharing that they feel as bored as I do sometimes, helping to give me some perspective that I'm not the only human being in the world who feels the way I do, it's great. And sometimes I can get into reading the literature, although my eyes glaze over when I try to read too much at a time. But it doesn't really last for me past the meeting, past the moment when it's actually going on. I'm worried. Because, damn it, a drink's looking better all the time. And even though I managed to hold on to my job when I drank, I still wrecked my life on booze. Lived like a pig. Felt like garbage. Life was hell." Leroy pauses. "But it *was* dramatic. Maybe that's what I miss. The drama. The threat of something about to collapse. That's when I know I'm alive—when I'm in a state of total panic or despair." Leroy shakes his head. "What a hell of a way to live."

Leroy squirms a little, as if deciding whether to divulge something else. He shrugs and sighs, then continues. "I used to go to prostitutes when I got drunk. Never had a normal relationship with a woman—you know, like meet some nice woman and go to dinner and have a few dates and then maybe go to bed with her. I guess I never felt good enough for that. But I liked paying for sex. A sale is something I understand. When I could turn it into merchandise, it seemed like I deserved it. That was a big thing for me. Getting drunk and then paying to get laid. Now—well, the truth is, I still pay for sex, but not with whores anymore. I buy a lot of pornography. I got paranoid about AIDS. Now that I'm sober, I'm afraid to actually have sex with anybody, especially the ladies I spent time with before. But it's not the same. It's not the same at all. I'm ending up feeling worse then I ever did before. I guess that's what makes me feel most apart from everybody. The shame. There's this bottomless *shame* in the center of me, like if anybody found out who I really was, they'd gasp in horror."

Leroy's shame about the whole "real" person he feels he has had to hide from the public world is familiar to many of the second-year recoverers I've met—for that matter, it's familiar to many recovering people with any amount of time in sobriety. The shame we feel about these secret parts of ourselves can be devastating and debilitating, mostly because it feels like proof that we're unacceptable, that we couldn't possibly fit in with other, nicer, more "recovered" people. There are some parts of us, we're certain, we could never tell anyone about.

And yet, as Leroy is beginning to discover right now, that doesn't have to be true.

"It does help to talk a little about it," he says after a moment. "It's funny to have it taken so seriously. And to feel I'm not being judged."

This tiny glimmer that he might be able to tug out his "secret self" a bit at a time has become a source of hope to Leroy. Since this conversation, he's decided to change sponsors, choosing someone who seems to have had some of the same "issues" Leroy has. "My new sponsor was the first man I ever heard talk in the rooms about feeling sexually obsessed," Leroy says, "and I can't tell you what it means to think I might actually have found someone I can talk to about this stuff." And at his new sponsor's suggestion, Leroy has also decided to try out a thera-pist, to see if he might experiment with telling the "truth" about himself in yet another context.

"I'm still jammed up about this stuff," Leroy says. "I'm not saying my boredom and my shame and everything else that drives me up a wall has gone away. But it really does help to be-gin to talk about more of it. And to see that nobody is laughing. Or running away from me. Or telling me I'll end up in hell. And, it's strange, I've actually gone through a few days where I don't lose the good feelings I get in meetings," Leroy smiles. "So maybe something is beginning to get better."

Realizing that even the most secret parts of you can be shared with someone else isn't something that comes quickly or com-pletely to most of us. But opening the door even a crack, letting even the barest amount of light in on what frightens us most about ourselves, can be wonderfully healing as well as illumi-nating. The clearest payoff is, once again, the sense that we don't have to keep ourselves apart from other people—or from re-covery. Sobriety seems to mean achieving connection and wholeness, integrating the "dark, secret self" with the public, "acceptable" one. Leroy has learned, simply by sharing some of his secrets with people he trusts, that you can start on the road to that wholeness any time you want. He's not sure where he'll end up. But when he makes the effort to "connect," it doesn't seem to matter quite as much as it used to. "Maybe, as I keep hearing in the program," Leroy says, "God will take care of the rest."

Dealing with the Wreckage and the Pain: Rebecca

Rebecca, unlike Leroy, doesn't feel she has any secrets. In fact, she says, "My life is an open book. It's a miserable, wretched story, but there are no secrets about it. You want to know what I have to put up with? What I feel in my soul about the whole stinking mess? Sit down for a few hours, and I'll tell you every gory detail. Only don't tell me, like AA or NA keep telling me, to keep turning it all over to God. God hasn't done a damned bit of good for me, as far as I can see."

When Rebecca, living in a small, "God-fearing" Washington town, even entertains the idea that there might *be* a God (which isn't often), her resentment threatens to burn her up: How could he/she/it have allowed her life to become such a painful mess? What did she do to deserve having to support a mother with Alzheimer's, deal with an abusive husband, and cope with the crippling, chronic pain of her rheumatoid arthritis? "Sobriety never promised me a rose garden," she says, "but couldn't it have given me something better than this?"

Rebecca says that in sobriety, which she hoped would bring her more serenity and acceptance, a better attitude to bring to all of the undeniable difficulties she must face day to day, she's simply gotten *more* angry. "At least it feels that way. I mean, I used to medicate myself with sleeping pills when I could afford them, and then cherry brandy. I told myself it was to lessen the pain of my arthritis. And to calm down when my husband got violent. To give me more patience with my mother, who's steadily going downhill with Alzheimer's. When one of my friends would ask me why I drank so much, I'd say because I can't afford tranquilizers. Tranquilizers—sleeping pills—were my favorite, really, when I had a job and I could get them from a willing doctor. But anyway, I never drank to get high. I drank to stop feeling the pain. With my disability I haven't been able to work; I used to be a short-order cook at a lunch place in town. And my husband is almost always out of work. Always getting into fights and getting fired. Now we're on welfare. And okay, I suppose we're a little better off financially than we were when money was going to the liquor store or the druggist every week, but in every other way things have gotten worse."

Rebecca says the main problem is she can't *escape* the way she used to. "It's like there's no safe place anymore. I do go to meetings. Usually I feel like an outsider; I hear people talking about their sick pets or that they bought the wrong material for their curtains and I want to say to them, Get *real!* But as much as I do let myself have an outburst now and then, even in an AA or NA meeting, I don't feel comfortable talking about my life in the rooms. I don't want to say the same things over and over. Who would want to hear it? That sometimes when I wake up I think I'll die from the pain in my hands and arms and knees. The pain that never really goes away, ever. Or that my husband has turned into a total growling stranger. Strange—he doesn't drink. His father was an alcoholic and he's made sure not to drink. But sometimes I wish he would! He's so demanding and nasty. I want to get a divorce, but where would I go, what would I do? And I'm afraid even to bring it up to him. I say he's abusive, and he is, verbally, but it's not like he hits me. At least not yet. But I'm too ashamed to talk about that again and again in the rooms. They all tell me to go to Al-Anon, even though my husband doesn't drink. It's likely they don't want to hear any more from me. And I don't blame them. . . ." Rebecca is close to tears. "And do you think I like sounding like a whiny brat? I hate sounding this way. I'd love my life to be different. But every day I wake up and feel this pain—not just the arthritis, but the pain of seeing things more clearly. It's like somebody turned on the light after it had been dark for ages, and after I get used to the shock and even the joy of being able to see, I'm in worse despair than ever. Because all I see around me is wreckage and pain. Who wants a life like this?"

Rebecca says she'd usually been able to spend afternoons with her mother and get some solace there. But her mother is drifting away irretrievably with the dementia caused by Alzheimer's. "She doesn't have any more money than I have. I dread putting her into a state-financed home. But what choice do I have?" The fact that her mother is slipping away seems symbolic to her. "It feels like every day the light dims in my mother's eyes, my hope dims too. I won't lie about it. There have been times I've thought of ending it all. I don't know how I'd do it. But killing myself isn't an impossible option. I wish something would come out of the sky and fix things. Tell me what to do. Give me money so I can put my mother in a decent home and live a decent life. Get away from my husband. I play the lottery. I'm embarrassed to say how much hope I place in the lottery! A lot more, to tell you the truth, than I've been putting in my 'Higher Power' lately. But the lottery isn't coming through for me either. . . ."

Nothing has come out of the sky to "fix things" for Rebecca. But recently, something did change. Hesitantly, she talks about it. "There was a woman who'd just moved to this part of the state who came into my Friday night AA meeting. It was a night when I decided to have one of my outbursts. The usual stuff: not only about my husband, and my mother, and my arthritis, and having no money, but how I just couldn't relate to people in the rooms who had 'luxury' problems. It angered me to hear people talk about such trivial stuff. I hadn't noticed this woman until after I spoke. She was sitting in the back. But she raised her hand after I was through with my tirade, said her name was Catherine, and thanked me for what I had to say. She said how much she identified. I wondered what she could be talking about. She was beautiful, well-turned out, looked like she had a lot of money—those clothes couldn't have cost nothing! She was young, probably in her early thirties. I'm working on fifty, and looking every minute of it! I know I should have felt good about someone saying they identified with me, but she was so pretty and looked so privileged that it just increased my resentment. Somehow I held myself back from blurting out, 'How could *you* know? You don't have any problems.' She didn't talk about herself, either, so as far as I knew she didn't have any. I was in a mood, anyway, to boil. This woman somehow just turned up the heat."

Then, at a break in the meeting when people got up for coffee and talked to one another for a few minutes, the pretty lady from the back of the room came up to talk with Rebecca. It was then that Rebecca realized she walked with a cane. From beneath Catherine's calf-length skirt, Rebecca could see a plastic prosthetic leg. Something in Rebecca shrank. She felt bad for thinking the things she'd thought about this woman. "Okay," Rebecca says she admitted to herself. "So maybe the woman *did* have some problems. Maybe even some big ones." But Rebecca still wasn't in the mood to open up. "I'd been through this sort of thing before," she says. "You know, the 'my boo-boo is worse than your boo-boo' thing that kids do with each other. What I've come to think of as the 'you think *you've* got problems!' syndrome. I wasn't in any mood to hear that this woman thought she was worse off than me. I didn't want to compare miseries."

But Catherine, as she took a seat next to Rebecca, didn't seem to want to engage in that kind of tug-of-war. What she said was simply this: "When you were talking, I was thinking what a good job you're doing, taking care of yourself and your mother in all that pain. It's a real power of example to me. Staying sober in the face of all that." Rebecca mumbled thanks, but privately felt a little uncomfortable. She wished the woman would go away. But Catherine continued: "You know what I've found myself doing? Every so often, no more really than a few moments here and there in the day, I tell myself, 'Boy, Catherine, you're doing a hell of a job. I like the woman you're becoming.'" Catherine laughed. "I'd never done that before! Now I feel I really mean it. And it's amazing how my day seems to lighten up a bit when I give myself that credit. I don't know why I wanted to tell you this. I guess just because I think you really deserve to feel good about yourself." Catherine smiled and said good-bye, got up to get some coffee, and went back to her seat. The meeting resumed.

Rebecca says she felt "unnerved. Catherine hadn't said anything I expected her to. She didn't tell me how hard it was for her to get through life on one leg. God knows what else was happening to her. But the strange thing was, I felt better. I realized I'd been living my life so defensively, so on guard, so ready to lash out at anyone who got in my way, that there was no real breathing space for me anymore. Life was such an ordeal partly because I expected it to be. I know that sounds a little Pollyanna. I mean, my problems are real, God knows. But Catherine helped me to see that maybe I'm not doing such a bad job after all. That maybe I deserve to give myself some credit."

Rebecca says this was a real moment of change for her. "Suddenly there seemed to be more space between me and what was going on in my life. I felt, maybe, like there might be a few more options than I was allowing myself to see. And one of them I could experiment with right off: feeling good about myself. About the way I'm handling all this responsibility, pain, and difficulty without picking up."

None of the troublesome externals have changed yet in Rebecca's life—except that she got Catherine's phone number and they now talk to each other on a regular basis. But her attitude has changed. She's allowed a new kind of contact between herself and the world, one that isn't quite so automatically hateful and defensive and fearful. One that allows her to breathe a little more freely, be kinder to herself, and reach out to other people, like Catherine, for understanding. "It's like," Rebecca sums up, "I've found a sort of small tap of love. And I've learned to turn it on a trickle. The world is still a difficult, painful place. But it's not as threatening and unmanageable as before. Something is softening in me. I don't hate so much anymore. And, for the moment, life is more livable."

No dramatic changes in outer life are necessary for the kind of transformation Rebecca speaks of. But it is the experience of many recovering people, as they progress from year one to year two to year three of sobriety (and on) that, with varying degrees of speed and completeness, the outer circumstances of life *do* end up changing. In fact, Rebecca has come up with what she thinks of as a crucial realization about this. "I see that much of what's going on in my outer life is a reflection of what's going on within me. When I feel hateful toward someone, it's not surprising if I get a hateful response back. Certainly that fuels my husband's nasty moods. I'm not saying my life is my fault. That's presumptuous: Who knows why we're given the challenges in life we're given? But there is a connection between how I feel and how my life turns out at the surface. I don't understand it, really. Catherine tells me it's enough to have discovered it's *there.*"

A Tale of Two Kittens: Jeffrey

Jeffrey, a Londoner, remembers hearing only one line of advice from his gruff and unloving father: "There's nothing a shot of whiskey and common sense can't cure." He finds himself so emotionally repressed, so self-hating, so full of buried anger that he can barely face himself in the mirror in the morning, much less chirp the Serenity Prayer.

"I accept that alcohol and drugs were destroying me," Jeffrey says. "But I still have so much difficulty with Twelve Step programs. Americans are so damned *cheerful.* They're like a bunch of eager little puppy dogs, I sometimes think. Either that or they're so damned earnest and sincere that you long for a good dose of gloomy Harold Pinter. All their damned 'issues.' And sometimes all this Twelve Step stuff seems just too American to be borne." Jeffrey shifts uneasily, looks apologetic. "I've always been a terrible snob, and I'm afraid I still have the reflex to be one. It seems some cruel twist of fate that I find I actually need to go to AA or NA meetings. As much as I find it distasteful, they're the only things that keep me from wanting to throw myself off a bridge."

Lately, even AA and NA haven't worked well. "The main thing about meetings, for me," Jeffrey says, "is that they give me someplace to listen to other people and, when the spirit moves me, to speak about my own life. Generally, I do feel some kind of connection, some kind of camaraderie, which I don't have to tell you is rare enough in English life. It is not 'done' to tell all your secrets to a roomful of strangers. And being gay as well as English, I've got a double dose of feeling I can't let anyone on to who I really am. I'm not alone in this. Meet just about any Englishman in my position, and you'll get a similar tale of woe. But it is woeful. And, frankly, I've begun to think that the culture and psychological stuff in the center of me runs so deep and is so unmanageable that I can't truly surrender it. I don't know how to get *rid* of it. I wish there were some operation, some surgical procedure I could undergo to get this horrible feeling I've got about myself taken out. Just cut it out. Maybe a lobotomy would work."

What precisely was it he wanted to cut out?

"The feeling that no matter what I do, no matter what Step I work, no matter how hard I try to follow the suggestions in the program, I'm still basically a shit. You can't dress this boy up and make him anything other than what he started out being: a worthless failure. I can't bear to look at myself. I don't think I'll *ever* do a Fourth Step. I can't possibly get into a relationship; now that I'm through my first year and into my second year, technically I'm 'allowed' to start thinking about relationships, but, God, who would want me in his life? I snipe at people. I can't seem to say anything that isn't cutting or hurtful or snide. This was all right when I drank. I mean, you were supposed to be cutting when you drank. We've got all this Oscar Wilde and Noel Coward tradition to live up to. But now—well, what's most painful about it is that I can't escape what the real feeling is. The problem isn't not liking *you*. It's not liking *me*. It's *loathing me*. And I can't seem to get past it."

The roadblock that Jeffrey perceived to any kind of satisfying life in sobriety seemed as impassable to him as the roadblocks faced by Leroy and Rebecca seemed to them. Like them, he felt in some sense unreachable, so constitutionally apart from the world that he couldn't imagine ever forging a real, much less nurturing, connection to it. But, also like Leroy and Rebecca, he has recently experienced something that's enabled him to see at least the possibility of making that connection.

"It amounts to this," Jeffrey explains. "I've inherited two eight-week-old kittens." Jeffrey blushes slightly. "This is the silliest thing, really. I never had a cat in my life, never wanted one. Now I've got two!" Jeffrey laughs. "What happened was, the friend of a man I know in AA had to move suddenly, and while he could take one animal, the mother of the two I've got, he just couldn't manage the kittens. My friend—well, I suppose he's more an acquaintance, really; I don't have anyone I'd call a real 'friend' in AA yet—this guy somehow got it into his head to ask me if I wanted kittens. And the damnedest thing happened. I thought about it for a moment, and some unaccustomed wild idea hit me that I *did* want them. I can't imagine why I said yes, but I did. And so now I'm learning to deal with two tiny frightened souls who so far have spent most of their waking hours hiding in the most preposterous nooks and crannies—kittens are ingenious at finding little dark holes in the wall, you've really got to watch out for them—when they're not chasing each other around or nibbling at my toes. I'm not completely out of my depth. But," Jeffrey said, smiling, "I'm also amazed. I love these two little fellows. Especially one of them."

Jeffrey says he's wary of playing favorites; his father had clearly preferred Jeffrey's older brother, Tom, to Jeffrey when they were little. ("Tom was the rugby star, the all-round real man, about as different as you could get from quiet little bookish me.") But he's irresistibly drawn to the kitten he calls "Cat One." "I can't imagine naming animals things like Horace and

MooMoo and Piccadilly or whatever it is you're conventionally supposed to name cats; as far as I can see, the cats don't give a damn what they're called. So I keep things simple. Cat One and Cat Two—One and Two for short." "One" is called that because he's always the first out of whatever crevice the kittens have managed to get themselves into. But he's also, as Jeffrey says, "like an alcoholic. My heart goes out to him, really. He's always the one pushing for the most food. He runs away the quickest, comes out first. He's just simply *louder* than Cat Two. Every emotion is outsized. When he cries, you feel the universe is imploding. When he's happy, he purrs so that you can hear him across the room. He wants, he wants, he wants. Cat Two, on the other hand, is content to sit there most of the time blinking at Cat One, as if to say, 'Oh, isn't he a handful. I can't imagine what you're going to do with *him*.'"

Jeffrey becomes self-conscious for a moment. "You don't know how rare it is for me to feel anything like this," he says. "Such joy. Such a kind of release, even a sort of sweetness inside me. And I suppose the real dividend is that, for the first time, I don't feel so completely self-obsessed, self-absorbed. By adding two little darts of life, two little streaks of orange and gray into my life—Cat One is a brilliant orange stripe, Cat Two a demure gray with bits of white—I'm just not so powerfully bound up in myself anymore. And, do you know, I caught myself looking at my reflection in the mirror the other day and I did not wince. I actually *did not wince*. I'm not saying I was about to pucker up or anything. But the reflexive self-hate had gone. That, to me, is an indescribable miracle."

We've introduced you to three people who were convinced there was no way out of their negative feelings and circumstances, not even in sobriety. It's clear from what second-year recoverers have shared with me that we don't experience "roadblocks" only when we drink. Sometimes we face some forbidding ones in sobriety too. And they can threaten to derail us just as dangerously as anything we faced drunk or high.

Just as clearly, second-year recoverers tell me there is no magical answer to getting past a roadblock. Whatever it is that allows you to shift the prism and see things from a different angle does not seem to be a matter of pure willpower. It's not that recovering people don't benefit enormously from using certain "tools"—the "Serenity Prayer," for instance—even at moments when they're convinced nothing will work. Sometimes merely considering what it means to "surrender" or what's "unmanageable" in your life, in other words, considering the First Step, can enable you to shift, to get that seemingly necessary distance from circumstances and overwhelmingly negative feelings that Rebecca spoke of. But there doesn't seem to be any one foolproof way to ensure that you'll forge a connection to the world in sobriety just at the moment you feel you need to.

Jeffrey, Rebecca, and Leroy all have told me that the bedrock decision they have somehow managed to stick to, *not picking up a drink or a drug no matter what happens or how they feel,* is finally what saves them. It saves them simply because it clears a space for their sober lives to happen. "Insight is impossible when you're blitzed" is how Jeffrey succinctly puts it. Rebecca says, "How can things get better when I'm killing myself with booze or drugs?"

But actually *letting in* the world, actually feeling what many recovering people can only call a spiritual sense of connection to life, to people, to themselves—and sometimes even to cats—seems to happen in unanticipated ways.

"I guess the only thing I know how to do," Leroy says, "is try to stay out of my own way. To remember that old AA saw, 'Feelings are not facts,' and not make my emotions push me in the direction of getting blotto." Rebecca adds: "Anything that gets me outside myself, even for a moment, helps me. What I need more than ever is more perspective about what's going on. Which really means more clarity. I can't deal with my life if my first response is to push it away." And Jeffrey: "I need to see I'm worthy. That sobriety is something I deserve and can enjoy. And like Cat One and Cat Two, that I might be able to live in the moment without *thinking* about it so damned much."

Lives are not neat: Lessons don't come prepackaged. And feelings, nobody has to tell you, don't follow any logical plan. What we've really been talking about are unmanageable feelings, ones that don't go away because you want them to. And most second-year recoverers teach me that they can be pretty horrendous: Kevin's isolation, Jeffrey's self-hate, Rebecca's resentments, and Leroy's boredom and loneliness aren't emotions limited to alcoholics and addicts, but they can threaten us in some particularly devastating ways.

What do other recovering people do when feelings like these come up? So much of the second year seems to mean facing these emotional corks in the ocean, these feelings that keep bobbing up again and again no matter how much you try to push them down. We can become exasperated: Why aren't we getting better? Why are these cravings and resentments still afflicting us? Why can't we let it go? *Why don't they just all go away?*

Dealing with what seem to be typically "second-year" feelings is such a crucial topic. Let's take a look at some strong, reassuring messages of hope from second-year recoverers who not only have managed to weather and learn from their emotional storms, but have allowed what they've learned to enrich the quality of their lives.

three

Emotional Storms:
From Danger to Self-Discovery

While there do seem to be differences between one year or stage of sobriety and another, it's equally evident that you end up having to deal with many of the same issues no matter what year you're looking at. You may now know that "feelings are not facts," but you still can feel awfully hobbled by resentment, fear, and anger. Feelings are still a hot topic in the second year. I often hear people with twenty years of sobriety dealing with many of the same emotional issues we have to face after one year of sobriety. What seem to change, slowly, are the *attitudes* we bring to those feelings.

Commonly, in the second year, we feel frustrated that despite our yearlong abstinence, our attempts to "work the program," and our boundless good intentions, we're still so often in the fierce grip of powerful, negative emotions. Sometimes our feelings seem to be even more overwhelming than they were in the days when we could blot them out with alcohol or drugs. The immediate danger may not be that we'll pick up a drink or a drug. The first danger is the feeling of separateness and abnormality we explored in the last chapter. Our emotional afflictions, as we may come to think of them, seem to separate us from the rest of the world, to make the prospect of recovery seem less likely as we become convinced that we're not like anybody else, and thus not susceptible to the same growth and promises of serenity and self-acceptance that other people seem to be able to acquire in sobriety.

Second-year recoverers also discover the idea of being gentler with themselves. They experience surprising moments of letting up on themselves and other people. They unearth a new tolerance. At these times, life does seem "softer"; in other words, less rigid, fearful, threatening. As one second-year recovering man, Alan, says, "I'm coming to think that my main task right now is to sort of clear the stage so that I've at least got the chance to live a sober life, a life that's not encumbered by fear and resentment. Another way of putting it is to allow myself to become receptive, which is trickier than I used to think it was. I can't *will* myself to be receptive. As my sponsor says, sobriety can't blast through a locked vault. Sobriety doesn't seem, in fact, to blast. It comes when it's beckoned, when it's truly wanted. Raging at ourselves for not being able to will serenity or self-acceptance into being is a good way of adding locks to the vault door."

What Alan says seems to be true: The world rarely yields to frontal assault. Or, as the poet W. H. Auden puts it:

> *Truth, like love and sleep, resents*
> *Approaches that are too intense . . .*

This is all very nice, you may be thinking, but the tidal wave of feelings can make it seem pretty lame—certainly not strong enough to withstand the fierce or debilitating emotions you can't avoid in day-to-day sobriety. You're also no longer a beginner dealing with these feelings. You've now had a year or more of living through them and dealing with them, without picking up a drug or a drink. All of which means you know a little about the subject yourself. But if you're like the majority of second-year recoverers I've listened to, you may suffer periodic bouts of doubt, depression, and exhaustion over the "ongoingness" of feelings, or for that matter, of life.

Susan, a young woman in AA with thirteen months of sobriety, put it like this: "I went through life thinking the whole point was to get to the next payoff, with each payoff being better than the last. Elementary school to junior high to high school to college: a clear ladder upward, as many A's as you could get, as many diplomas, all taking you to the next even more terrific stage. That's how I drank too. Each high had to be better than the last. Each man I met had to be a step up. Everything had to be better, more, higher and higher, till you got to some incredible Prize in the Sky, till you were so famous and rich and satiated that you could—what? Die, I guess.

"But now life seems so different. It just is. My main task is simply to face the moment at hand. I have a different relationship to my dreams. I still have dreams, but now that I'm sober, I find I don't expect them to come true in the wild way I did when I was drunk. Now I sort them out to see what they're telling me, trying to intuit direction from them in a much more thoughtful way. Sometimes that's okay. But other times I want to scream at the slowness of everything! I go into a state of euphoric recall, and I can only remember the great times when I was drunk, the all-night clubs, the wild music, the time this major record executive picked me up and we went to his penthouse in his limo, the times when it seemed the world was there for the taking. . . . Then I 'wake up' and remember the horror, the despair, the complete wreckage of the last years of my drinking, what it did to my life, to my spirit. And I return to the present. To what I'm going to make for dinner. To feeding the dog. To picking up my laundry. I feel sometimes like I've been blasted by alcohol—that now, even after more than a year of sobriety, I still have to take things very slowly and carefully and attend to each small detail of my life, not worrying about the big stuff, about the huge grand arc of my future. But it's hard. Those dreams, that crazy wild abandon of the best part of my drinking life, were terrific. There are times I hate having to give them up."

The Ache for High Drama

Susan illustrates a number of themes that come up a lot for people in their second year of sobriety, and that may have already come up in the first year and may continue into the third and fourth and fifth years of sobriety!

Sometimes our yearning for the "good old days" is not just a result of euphoric recall, the selective tendency of memory to pick out all the good times and conveniently forget the bad. Our attraction to misery can be just as potent. Andrew, who has fourteen months of sobriety, says, "I never felt really alive unless I was miserable. I think it was how I knew I existed. On the verge of getting thrown out of my apartment for nonpayment of rent, my girlfriend dumping me, my boss about to fire me, and me tragically wasted on booze and drugs, the misunderstood loner, the guy who always got the butt end of life—this whole idea that I was a victim of Fate was enormously alluring. It meant I was a kind of noble figure, marked by tragedy over which I had no power." Andrew smiles. "What a crock. But I didn't think it was a crock then. It was how I defined myself. And the great jagged peaks of my misery—God, it was like my life was some kind of mysterious, dramatic novel or movie. I was the tragic star. Someday they'd understand. Someday they'd discover me, like they discovered Van Gogh after his death; they'd discover what a gem of a human being I was. What a misunderstood genius. I got a lot of mileage out of thinking of myself like that."

This hunger for drama, for seeing ourselves as larger than life whether the outsize vision is full of misery or of elation, is common for recovering people, and never more than in the second year of sobriety. The absence of that glamour can leave us feeling baffled and unfulfilled in sobriety. We think, "What is there to aspire to? Simply not drinking and drugging one day at a time for the rest of my life? That doesn't sound like much of a life. . . ."

Andrew says he's realized that sometimes, to compensate for his lost "tragedy," he tends to "sabotage things, almost just to make them interesting. Something starts going well at my job or with a woman I've just met and I'll do something to screw things up. I won't come through at the last minute; I'll miss a deadline or not show up at the time I said I would. It adds drama, somehow, as well as a dose of the old tragic misery I seemed to thrive on in my drinking life. I want my life to have *spice,* dammit. I'm not sure serenity is such a terrific idea, at least not my notion of it. I want glory and high emotions and impossible dreams. Not simply to face another bowl of oatmeal in the morning."

Andrew identifies a crucial role that strong emotions seem to play for second-year recoverers, as well as people in earlier and later stages of sobriety: feelings acting as *distraction.* We may turn to the power of feelings the way we used to turn to alcohol or drugs. It's no secret, for example, that anger acts like a drug on the body: Rage gets adrenaline flowing, and this chemical change in the body can feel very much like a "high." Many people in the first years of sobriety find themselves getting addicted to exercise too, especially to running. "I became fanatic about it, and I couldn't understand why," says Carolyn, who has a year and a half of sobriety, "until I went for a doctor's appointment and he told me in passing that running was a good way to release endorphins in the body—the chemicals that cause the brain to feel pleasure. Boy, did I feel like an addict. I was killing myself running to get high, really. It's fascinating the lengths I'll go to alter my consciousness!"

Strong emotions are, in recovering people's experience, a lot like strong drugs. They *alter* us; they give us at least a hint of the entirely changed consciousness we regularly sought and found through alcohol and drugs. It's no wonder that so many of us feel addicted to high drama. What we're experiencing at these moments is often literally a chemical rush. We train our bodies to provide themselves with drugs.

Is the implication, then, that we should avoid strong emotion at all costs? Because it's dangerous to get high, no matter how "naturally" we accomplish it?

The first truth about feelings is that we couldn't avoid them even if we wanted to. Sobriety does not mean becoming less human. And it is entirely human to feel the full range of emotions, from rage to elation. Rather, it seems that our task as recovering people is to become conscious of what our emotions are doing to us, to create the "space" that Rebecca talked about between us and the raging storm. Not that this detachment is easily achieved, or that we can't recover from the storm of our emotions even when we don't achieve detachment. Nowhere in sobriety are more mistakes made than in the area of our feelings.

Susan says, "Sometimes I'm good at seeing what's causing my emotional storm and I can put a little distance between me and my fear or anger or resentment. I can choose not to act out self-destructively, or say or do something hurtful to somebody else. But sometimes I just lose it. Like when my landlord is ignoring my phone calls about the leaks in the bathroom, and I know he's listening to his damned answering machine because I can hear him walking around his apartment, which is just under mine. I am not above going downstairs and pounding on his door, screaming bloody murder at him. Not that I'm especially proud of this behavior. But—hey, I live in the real world. Sometimes you get nuts. I suppose what I *am* trying to do, even after an explosion like that, is pick up the phone and talk about it to my sponsor. Because even if I can't get the right distance from my emotions at the moment they're happening, I can always try to get some perspective on them later. That's what I heard the Tenth Step is about: giving you the chance to look at cause and effect, at the consequences of your actions, and seeing if there's anything you want to change about your behavior."

Susan says that she has no doubt that giving in to her "emotional storms" does something else for her. "When I really look at how I react to things, at how I sometimes let my feelings take over my behavior, I almost always see that there's something I'm trying to avoid, and that acting out on my feelings becomes a kind of excuse not to look at what's really bothering me. For instance, that landlord thing. It's not that he's not a jerk—he is. But when I thought about it later, I saw that I was so hungry to feel self-righteous, to explode at somebody who was clearly in the wrong when I was clearly in the right, because I wasn't feeling very good about other stuff I *wasn't* right about. Like I've been putting off completing this report my boss asked me to have on her desk two weeks ago. I haven't really even started it yet. I've been feeling so guilty and lazy and incompetent that I realize I was spoiling for a fight, for some situation in which I could prove that I was the martyr and the good girl and the one sinned against. My rage was really a distraction, something to keep me from looking at what I really needed to do. And of course it also got me high—that old chemical adrenaline rush. But it also got me hung over.

"That's something I haven't mentioned. As much as I fall on opportunities to feel self-righteous like a starving animal, I never feel good about myself afterward. Every time I get into a tug-of-war between the good guys and the bad guys, every time I seek to blame somebody else for everything that's going wrong in my life, I always end up feeling a little unclean, almost. Some deeper part of me knows I'm not facing the truth. That I'm escaping, the way I used to escape into alcohol and drugs, what's really going on, what's really at issue. And I get stymied. Self-righteousness turns to self-hate. That's when I've got to pick up the phone or go to a meeting. To discover that what I'm going through are the perfectly normal paces of any recovering addict and alcoholic. And I can start to feel better about myself too. That at least I'm trying to be conscious of what my emotions mean in my life. It never occurred to me to ask the first question about them before, when I was drunk. So, that's progress. And it relieves me to know that I'm still sort of on track."

Susan has just described an "arc" of facing and dealing soberly with strong emotions that can be seen as a model for the way many other recovering people deal with similar emotions. It begins with the appeal of self-righteous indignation and the chemical rush of giving in to the "storm," which gives way to a kind of hungover withdrawal from that storm, followed by a thoughtful consideration of what was really going on and what the "storm" might really have been covering up. We move from a kind of impenetrable, dramatic darkness into the first glimmers of conscious light. At the best times, we eventually become a little clearer about what we're doing to ourselves in our emotional storms, and how we might change what we do to ourselves the next time they threaten us.

But some emotions run so deep that they aren't susceptible to a quick Tenth Step analysis, or, sometimes, at least at first, even to an in-depth Fourth Step investigation. And these emotions are often attached to a deep and complicated web of secrets—secrets that may cause feelings of shame or embarrassment or self-censure, but secrets that won't go away. Many addicts and alcoholics admit to feeling plagued by an overactive fantasy life, one that can intrude with devastating effects in sobriety. Now that we're no longer drunk or high, we sometimes feel deprived, and may turn to our fantasies with a new desperation, seeking in them something of the release we used to find in drugs or alcohol. It's a whole "secret" area that many second-year recoverers find themselves needing to face with some urgency.

Sobriety, as many people in their second year discover, "wants" to shed light on everything, including these dark and sometimes fearful areas. Fortunately, the experience of allowing even a little light to fall on what you find most secret about yourself is almost always vastly more healing than you ever imagined it could be.

The Tyranny of Fantasy:
Facing Your Secrets

We've already seen, in Leroy's story, that it can be wonderfully healing to shed a little light on the "dark" parts of ourselves we thought we had to keep hidden: the memories, traits, secret desires, and embarrassments that make us feel most ashamed and fearful about anyone getting to "really" know us. Often some of the worst memories are those from our drinking and drugging days. With inhibitions more or less blasted out by booze or drugs, it's the rare addict and alcoholic who didn't get into some pretty colorful and disturbing trouble.

As I canvassed second-year recoverers, however, it wasn't the lurid "tell-all" secrets that seemed to rankle most. The "outrageous" sexual escapades, stealing, hiding, sneaking, tearing your clothes off in the middle of the party, losing control over your bowels or bladder at supremely inopportune moments. These experiences are undoubtedly painful to remember, but because they are all more or less the direct result of being drunk or high, we can understand them as clear manifestations of the disease of addiction. About many of these incidents we have no trouble saying, "It wouldn't have happened if I hadn't been drunk or high."

It's the deeper secrets, the parts of us that aren't so clearly manifestations of disease, that seem to cause the most trouble. The secrets that don't go away, the parts of us that remain even after we've stopped drinking or drugging: These are what can be terrifying. When we hear that some alcoholics and addicts are "constitutionally incapable of being honest with themselves," many of us quake a bit: Are any of us ready to be *completely* honest about who we are?

After a year or more of sobriety, it's common for these difficult secrets to make themselves more uncomfortably known, to intrude more painfully into consciousness. Brenda, a freelance actress in her mid-fifties, describes her own progress from a kind of insulated first year of sobriety to a far less comfortable second year: "When I stopped doing cocaine and drinking wine, I felt steamrolled: The world was so shockingly new, and I felt so completely unmoored by not having my usual doses of alcohol and drugs that it was all I could do to get through the day. I honestly didn't care about anything but staying sober. And that was so wonderful, because I actually gave myself permission to pay attention to myself, to my sobriety, to doing the next simple right thing. I did almost no acting work; I went to temping, which just about any freelance actor has to do some of the time, then I went to a meeting, sometimes AA, sometimes NA, then came home and usually had take-out or frozen food with my husband—it was beyond me to cook that first year!—and went to bed. Life was blissfully simple. But it's not simple anymore. Because more of 'me' than I'm used to dealing with keeps coming up."

Brenda had been in therapy for years before getting sober, and she had, on what she called a "cognitive, intellectual level," begun to deal with some of her "demons." "I've always known I had an overwhelming fantasy life. I have no doubt it's why I'm so attracted to acting. Movies were like heaven to me: the way things *ought* to be. Beautiful men and women acting out noble tragedies. There wasn't a thirties or forties Bette Davis movie I didn't know by heart! I know that a lot of people, and heaven knows a lot of actors, feel that way about Hollywood fantasies. We all lost ourselves at the movies! My problem was that I could never come *out* of these fantasies. The 'real world' was intolerable to me. And to block out the real world, I drank and drugged. Drinking loosened me up, helped me to have a sense of humor— or at least that's what it did for about the first ten years. Then it just started getting me drunk. To counteract the down effect of alcohol, I discovered cocaine. Boy, was cocaine a find! It convinced me, for the first time in my life, that I could conquer the 'real' world. I'd storm into agents' offices demanding jobs. I'd break into soliloquies at the least provocation, intent on proving what an extraordinary actor I was. It fed right into the Bette Davis fantasy, really: I could do anything if I really tried. Unfortunately, before long the only thing cocaine enabled me to achieve was a prolonged state of paranoia. I became convinced that studio executives were out to get me. They'd plant spies in the waiting rooms of every place I went to audition. Cocaine was making me even crazier than I was before. So, sometimes, I'd try for the old 'loose' effect of wine. But alcohol didn't do anything but make me pass out. My life swung between two extremes: unconscious on wine, or hyperalert and terrified on cocaine."

Brenda just barely managed to hold on to her marriage throughout those last chaotic years of her drinking and drugging. "My husband just about had it with me," she says. "Finally, he went into therapy and was convinced by his therapist that Al-Anon might be a good idea. Therapy I could understand, but Al-Anon? It got to me, even in my whacked-out state, that he wouldn't be resorting to Al-Anon unless he thought his wife was a mess. God, that was painful. But something penetrated. Maybe I *was* an addict and an alcoholic. Maybe I really needed help."

Brenda had long ago stopped seeing her old therapist, but she called her up again; their conversation ultimately led her to a rehab and her first AA and NA meetings. She also began going back to therapy. Now she's nearing two years of sobriety in AA and NA, and in "sober" therapy.

"It's terrific having this much time sober," Brenda says. "But it's also confusing. And sometimes frightening. As I said, earlier sobriety was easier because all I did was take the simplest measures to stay sober. My fear of the world lifted a bit: I simply didn't *care* as much what people thought about me in those early weeks and months. But now—" Brenda sighs. "That old fantasy life is starting to come back with a vengeance. It isn't easy to talk about. But sometimes I feel these huge upwellings of desire for other men, men other than my husband. I just want something dramatic to happen—some wonderful swept-away feeling of falling in love again. The hard truth is, now that I'm sober, I feel romantically indifferent to my husband. In fact, I resent him for not being Gerard Depardieu. This may sound funny and trivial, but it's not. You don't know how close I've come to placing a personal ad like 'sexy middle-aged married woman seeks lover on the side'; how close I've come to propositioning men I see in the street! And maybe the worst part is I'm starting to long for wine again, and maybe some cocaine too. Sometimes I'm convinced, hey, I've been off drugs and alcohol for nearly two years—what if I'm not an addict or alcoholic after all? What if I just needed a break to clear my head? The real ache, the real hunger is for something *overwhelming* to happen to me. And, more and more, it seems like there are two main obstacles to that: my husband and my sobriety."

It's gotten to the point with her husband, Brenda says, where "I simply freeze whenever he makes a sexual overture. Now I feel that I was only able to have sex with him before because I was drunk or high, not because of any real desire to be with him. All I know is that he's not my fantasy man. Every man I see in the street seems to be closer to that fantasy than he is! And the fantasy scares me, because it's so complete. I can get lost in it. I fantasize about being caressed and talked to in ways my husband never has. I imagine the man's voice, the life we'd have together, the fun I'd have with him, the complete understanding. . . . I know this may sound like a romance novel, but you don't know how strong and detailed it all is! It's taking over my life the way my acting fantasies did when I drugged and drank. It's all I can think about—finding and being with the perfect man, who's everything my husband isn't." Brenda sighs again. "It's so strange and painful to feel so sexually and romantically hungry, and yet not able to respond to my husband *at all.*"

The discomfort of all this has seriously tempted Brenda to go back to some kind of drug—maybe this time, she speculates, something for depression or anxiety that she could get "legitimately, prescribed by a doctor. . . . I do go through terrible bouts of depression. I mean, my husband is very hurt; he feels terribly rejected by me. We go through long discussions about it. But I don't have the guts to tell him the truth: that I can't stand him because he's not my perfect man. I feel like a petulant sixteen-year-old girl who doesn't like who asked her to the prom. Except that I'm a grown, married woman! The *hunger* I feel—there's no describing the strength of it. . . ."

Brenda has begun to talk about this with others, mostly her sponsor and her therapist. "It's helped a little. But there's something I'm still holding on to, something I'm still deeply afraid of, something so deeply rooted in me that I don't have a clue what it's really about. All I know is that I feel a tremendous amount of self-loathing. I can't *stand* that I can't get over these fantasies and this block against my husband. Why can't I have nice Donna Reed–type feelings? Why can't I be satisfied with the faithful, caring, attractive husband I've got? Why are these secret yearnings in me so compelling?"

The tyranny of our "secret selves" can be gut-wrenching. The second-year recoverers who have been able to reveal even parts of these secrets to me look and act as if they were tiptoeing carefully through a minefield: if they wander too indiscriminately or too freely over this territory, they feel they'll set off a devastating explosion. There seems to be something extraordinarily potent and threatening about what we may think of as "the most secret parts" of ourselves.

However, now that Brenda has broken her silence about her secret fantasies, she's discovered something peculiar. "My sponsor, Claire, helped me to see things a little differently. She told me that, when I described the fantasy man and life that haunted me so strongly, she kept getting the image of exotic, hothouse flowers—blooms that I secretly nurtured, secretly cherished, and yet kept completely secret from everyone. That gave me a clue. Maybe the problem was the *secrecy.* Maybe the problem was that I thought I had to hate my fantasies because I'd judged them as inappropriate, self-indulgent, immoral, stupid, or impracticable. Hating them kept them painful. And hating how unresponsive I felt about my husband kept my unresponsiveness exactly where it had always been: in the threatening dark.

"But the image of my fantasies and secret thoughts as flowers: that was a revelation. Maybe they were something precious! They weren't there for no reason. They were there because of who I was. And if I hated them, how could I help but hate myself? Maybe I had to take a whole new tack with them. Maybe I might actually have to accept that I have them. *Acceptance.* That's what had always been missing. I'd been protecting these hothouse flowers so assiduously, and yet hating them at the same time. No wonder I was miserable. No wonder I've felt so divided."

Accepting her fantasies and her feelings doesn't mean that she especially wants to keep them, Brenda says. "But I'm giving myself *permission* to have them. Not act out on them, necessarily, but to have them. After all, what choice have I got? They'll be there whether I want them to be or not. But the real illumination for me is that something's starting to lift a bit. My self-hate. I still don't feel a miraculous new desire to have sex with my husband, but I'm not so afraid of him anymore, or of my own responses to him. Something is softening. Something is getting better."

The self-acceptance Brenda is moving toward has already begun to have a healing effect. As she grows to accept her "hothouse flowers," she's developed a new attitude of permissiveness, of allowing herself to feel and be who she is. This permissiveness has a dividend: She feels more "sober" as a result of accepting herself more. "I feel like I've applied the First, Second, and Third Steps to my fantasies. I've surrendered to my powerlessness over them, and there's a new belief—which quite astonishes me—that something more powerful than me might restore me to some kind of clarity or sanity about all this. And God knows I feel the heartfelt desire to turn it over."

More Rewards of Opening Up

Carolyn has also harbored a secret she hasn't been able to let her sponsor know until recently. "The truth is," Carolyn says, "I've put on sixty pounds since I stopped taking drugs and drinking. I can't seem to stop eating. I'm so ashamed of myself; I didn't go to my fifteenth-year high school reunion. I couldn't bear to have anyone see me like this! I do get some reassurance from other people in AA and NA who say they've gone through this, that I should be gentle with myself, just concentrate on sobriety, put this on the shelf, but it's been more than a year now and the shelf is getting as heavy as I am!

"Anyway, the real secret is—well, I got to such a point of despair that I decided to start taking some of those over-the-counter diet pills. I mean, it probably sounds foolish to anyone who's not an addict or alcoholic: What's wrong with taking a mild appetite suppressant? In fact, my mother takes them, and since I've gained all this weight, she's been pushing me to take them too. 'They're perfectly safe!' she keeps saying. But she doesn't know how it scares me. This is petty stuff, these caffeine pills, or whatever they are. But they remind me of when I was hooked on amphetamines, and while I don't feel the same buzz from these things, I don't feel *sober* either. I'm still *taking something*. I've come to feel even more shame about taking diet pills than I do about being this heavy. Have I screwed up my sobriety? I mean, I take them as directed—but I have to say, I put so much hope into what I pray they'll do for me. It's like I'm desperate for a quick fix again—something to make me lose weight overnight. That's how I felt when I drugged and drank. I would take anything that promised to 'fix' me, quick. I feel such despair over all this. . . ."

It's not the purpose of this book to pass judgment on Carolyn's behavior; rather, the intention is merely to open up what is to so many recovering people a frightening Pandora's box, to show that it can be, in fact probably should be, opened. As Carolyn says, "It was only when I was able to talk about this with my sponsor that I felt I had the chance of dealing with any of it. My sponsor allowed me to see that I was trying to block out my hunger instead of find something that would truly feed it, just the way I did when I took amphetamines. My hunger isn't for food. I know that, rationally. I've just been eating by reflex. What I'm starting to feel and see now is that I've been misinterpreting my hunger. It's as if I can't stand even the tiniest hint of discomfort; I'm so afraid of the pain of it, that my reflex is still to do anything I can do to get rid of it. First it was food; now that I've gotten so fat, I'm searching for a quick fix like the amphetamines I used to take to ease the pain of being fat. It's never-ending. Or at least it doesn't end until I stop and talk about it with someone else. Then, at least, there's a chance of making what I'm doing *conscious*—not just something clung to out of fear and desperation, with all kinds of self-hate as the 'reward.' God, it's exhausting, sometimes. But *talk about it.* That's what I've always got to do. That's the beginning of getting better."

What Carolyn is discovering in "talking about it" is that there isn't any naysayer in the sky (or on the earth) ready to pounce on her for her least indiscretion. "Lightening bolts don't seek me out because I've done something 'terrible.' Neither—and this is more amazing—do my sponsor or my friends in NA judge me. In fact, I'm starting to hear so many other recovering people deal with equally difficult stuff, other addictive behaviors they can't seem to give up."

Many of us in the second year of sobriety begin to discover that we're tied to a lot more behaviors than the one we entered a Twelve Step program to change. The growing realization that we're still hooked to something—food, nicotine, sex, work, credit cards, gambling, or whatever else—can be devastating. The second year often marks the first time we begin to take a look at these behaviors, or at least to acknowledge that we feel in their grip. As Carolyn says, it's immensely healing to realize that nobody's waiting in the wings to judge us for these behaviors, whatever they are. In fact, most of us identify very strongly with people who are struggling with other addictive issues. That's another reassurance: You're far from alone if you come to feel you're "multiaddicted."

Ed is a recovering man in AA who's just begun to grapple with his ongoing attachment to having anonymous sex, simply by acknowledging it: "I've at least opened up the subject with my sponsor," he says. He relays something he heard in an AA meeting that's helped him a lot: "Deal with your addictions in the order in which they'll kill you." "I tried to give up smoking, caffeine, sugar, and sex, and pay the IRS back, when I hit my first-year anniversary," Ed says. "Within two weeks I was ready to pick up a drink. I kept beating myself up for not being perfect. And I totally forgot that I *had* managed to make it through a year without drinking. Somehow that didn't seem important anymore. I'd forgotten that it was the central miracle of my life! I'd learned not to kill myself with the one thing that threatened me the most: alcohol. Now I've started to realize how important a gift and triumph it is that I'm able to stay abstinent from alcohol. Whenever I beat myself up for something else I'm not doing perfectly, I try to remind myself that I'm still sober in AA. And nothing I do need take away from that."

We need to learn, as both Ed and Carolyn have, that the best beginning we can make is to reveal what is tearing us up inside to someone we can trust. And certainly discretion seems to be important. "I don't feel comfortable talking about a lot of my 'issues' in the rooms," Ed says, "especially the sexual ones. But I find as long as I get them out to *somebody*—like my sponsor— the pressure lets up, at least a little. Eventually I may be able to go to Sexual Compulsives Anonymous. Eventually I may be able to give up smoking. I've already gone to a few Twelve Step meetings on quitting smoking, and I think I'll go back. But thank God I don't *have* to do anything today but not drink. I have to trust that all the rest of the stuff in my life will get worked on as I'm able to work on it. Staying sober, which means, first of all, not drinking and going to meetings, has to be my definition of success right now."

There are no rules about what point in your sobriety you "should" decide to seek help for other addictive problems you may feel you have. Carolyn can't quite bring herself to attend Overeaters Anonymous, although she's talking about it with her sponsor and expects she'll start going to meetings someday. Ed hasn't felt ready to commit himself to Sexual Compulsives Anonymous. From my observations, Carolyn and Ed are typical of many second-year recoverers: In our second year, it's often enough simply to broach difficult issues. You can't start to deal with something before you've allowed yourself to see it. Many of us at least start to "see it" in our second year, laying the groundwork for further exploration in subsequent years.

But whatever our stage of sobriety, or of dealing with our other addictive behaviors, it seems essential to reinforce and feel good about the sobriety we do have. Ed says, "My sobriety is exactly that: *mine.* I'm the one who's got to be comfortable with all this. It really doesn't matter what anybody else thinks or says. Not that it's not a good idea to listen to what other people have to say. But when they start judging me, I'm learning that they're out of bounds. Just as I've had to learn that I'm out of bounds when I start to judge them back."

And Carolyn: "My sponsor has helped me to see that the person who got up the earliest today is the one who's got the most sobriety. She's told me about other people who have had ten or fifteen years and then gone out—and not come back. They're worse off now than they were when they came into the program. Being sober really means coming back *every day*. It's not like getting a diploma from school or a marriage license or something. Sobriety isn't something you get branded with, a label you get that makes you sober for the rest of your life. I'm discovering I have to renew my sobriety about as often as I have to breathe. It's something I have to be conscious of all of the time. And, surprisingly, it's not a chore being conscious of it. Because being conscious of sobriety means being conscious of *me*, of what's going on in my life. It means a new clarity."

The process of facing and deciding to reveal your secrets seems to be a lifelong one. As the people you've met in this section make clear, it's also immensely healing. Amazingly, it doesn't mean what your worst fears may once have told you it meant: opening yourself to somebody's horrendous judgment, whether God's or your sponsor's. Telling the truth about yourself seems to be healing because it's telling *yourself* the truth. As Brenda says, "It's the clarity that's so wonderful now. Facing how I really feel, that it's okay to be exactly where I am and feeling exactly what I do feel, is unbelievably freeing. It's not that I can expect everyone to approve. My husband and I still have problems. I still don't quite feel I can open up to him. And I'm even facing the prospect that I may not be able to do so for a very long time. But we're on a new footing. We're being *loving* to each other. Who thought that could happen, in the face of all my 'terrible' secrets? But we are. And we are because we're learning not only that we can't help being who each of us is, but that it's *okay* to be who we are. Of course, what we do with this information is important too. But I've learned that I don't have to act precipitously. I don't have to run out and *do* anything right now. I'm still working on two years of sobriety, for heaven's sake. I'm still trying to get emotionally sober, working on staying sober every day of my life. That's a big order right there. The rest of my life—

well, it will have to turn out however it does. All I pray is that I won't hate myself as all of this unfolds. And that I try to remain as conscious, honest, and kind as I can, no matter what happens."

What we've been seeing in everyone we've met so far in this book are different variations of "opening": admitting some feeling of connectedness with the world, with other people, and then finding ways to reinforce that feeling of connection. According to the second-year recoverers I've met, beginning the process of facing and then sharing your secrets with someone else is one way of forging that connection. But there are other ways as well.

It's common for recovering addicts and alcoholics in their second year to begin to reach out to the world in more formal ways. One version of this formal reaching out is called "service" in Twelve Step programs. Service can mean any number of things, ranging from setting up chairs for a meeting and making coffee to becoming a sponsor. It can mean being the speaker at the meeting or acting as secretary or treasurer. It can also mean simply going to a meeting and sitting in a chair: the "service" of showing another recovering alcoholic or addict that you're there to fulfill the primary purpose in any Twelve Step program, which is to stay sober and help someone else stay sober. But whatever form it takes, service is something recovering people often find themselves doing more conscientiously in their second year. What they discover in the course of giving service is often filled with revelations.

Let's take a look at what some of those revelations can be.

fOUR

Service:
The Adventure of Reaching Out

"Any lingering delusion I may have had that AA was like Sunday school or a scout troop was blasted to hell at my first AA business meeting," says Jack, an advertising executive in Los Angeles who's been sober for about sixteen months. "That was the greatest loss of innocence I've ever experienced, whether before or after I stopped drinking." Jack grins. "Well, maybe I'm exaggerating a little." His grin disappears: "Then again . . ."

After Jack had been going to meetings for a year, his sponsor suggested that he get involved in some kind of formal AA "service." "My sponsor doesn't talk much," he says. "He didn't give me a whole list of wonderful reasons about camaraderie and the joy of getting involved and knowing that you were really helping people and learning about cooperation and all the other stuff that people talk about when they say how great it is to 'do service.' Mostly he just told me, 'Don't drink. Go to meetings.' He's the kind of sponsor who, if I gripe too much, tells me I don't have any real problems as long as I don't drink. Sometimes that exasperates me. Other times it sort of bursts my balloon, gets rid of anxiety, brings back some kind of perspective. Refreshing guy, my sponsor. So when he told me to start making coffee for my home group and go to a business meeting, it surprised me. It was the lengthiest and most specific advice he'd given me in a year."

Jack says he didn't mind the idea of going to a business meeting. He imagined it would be just a different kind of AA meeting, maybe more boring, what with agendas about how much literature to buy, or whatever it was they talked about. But he's gone to enough business meetings in his work life not to feel especially interested in or intimidated by the prospect of going to an AA version of one.

However, making coffee was a different kettle of grounds. "I have to admit, my ego got in the way of that one," Jack says. "I didn't say this to my sponsor or anything. After all, I'd heard enough about how important humility was in sobriety to know that it wouldn't go down real well to say I felt above making coffee at a meeting. And hell, it's not like I wasn't humbled by alcohol and drugs. Somehow I'd managed to perform well enough in my job to keep it, but everything else sucked. I was up to my ears in credit card debt, my wife and kids left me, I defaulted on my mortgage and ended up camping out in a tiny, messy studio apartment in West Hollywood with a woman I'd once had an affair with when she'd been my secretary. *We* were a piece of work, lemetellya, passed out every night on quaaludes and vodka."

Life, Jack says, had been hell. "And God knew I didn't have any illusions about being superior to anybody, or that I was anything but powerless over alcohol and drugs. But still—making coffee." Jack says he couldn't help wincing at the idea. "Even when I was drunk, once I got into the office I had secretaries and clerks who worked for me. I was still kind of a big shot, even when I was at my worst. Fact is, I'm used to running things. Getting other people to do what I tell them to do. So why hadn't my sponsor suggested that I do something more in keeping with my temperament and experience? I mean, I could imagine chairing an AA meeting, maybe. Or doing something else that made use of my managerial skills. But I wasn't a cook or a waiter." Jack

pauses for a moment as he recalls how he felt. "But the real secret was I was scared. The most embarrassing thing about it was
I didn't know *how* to make coffee. I'd never cooked anything in
my life. When I couldn't get a lover, my wife, or an assistant to
make something for me, including a cup of coffee, I lived on
take-out. This wasn't going to be a lesson in humility. This was
going to be *humiliating.*"

Perhaps you won't be surprised to hear that Jack ended up experiencing something quite different than he thought he would,
once he actually volunteered to help out with "hospitality." "My
sponsor had never steered me wrong before," Jack says, "and even
though I felt uncomfortable, I went ahead with it. Got there early
and met the 'hospitality person' whose job I was taking over. A
real nice young grad student from UCLA, quiet guy with glasses
who said he'd never had his nose out of a physics book until *his*
sponsor suggested he help out with the coffee at this meeting. He
knew exactly how I felt. In fact, when I realized it didn't take a genius to dump water in the coffee maker, put in the coffee basket,
cover the coffee maker and plug it in—I couldn't believe that was
all you had to do!—I had a few good laughs about it. But it ended
up being nice in another way. Other people came in with cookies,
put them in baskets with paper napkins, then we all set up chairs,
joking about what control freaks we all were. We each had separate ideas about how far apart the chairs should be spaced, that
sort of thing. But it was fun. We laughed a lot.

"In some ways, I felt more connected, doing this kind of service, than I ever had before in AA. I was actually *doing* something here—something very concrete. Though I did feel like a
nut case when the first people came into the room and headed
for the coffee urn. Would they like it? Was it strong enough? Hot
enough? Would they spit it out? Had I put in the right amounts
of water and coffee? Oh Lord, suddenly I was sure I hadn't!
Maybe I should have gotten a whole bunch of herb tea bags out
there, or more instant decaf. Why hadn't I thought to buy some

fresh fruit so they'd have an alternative to all those cookies? This was California, after all—a lot of people here were health food freaks. My mind was racing. Before the first cup of coffee had been poured, I'd made plans to revamp everything, put in ferns, have some nice, quiet New Age music in the background, supply whole-grain, all-natural breads, muffins, and pastries, and turn this into one of southern California's first and best Alcoholics Anonymous clubhouses, a twenty-four-hour cafe for recovering people!"

Jack laughs. "I'd never worried about stuff like this before! And then when somebody actually poured herself a cup of coffee, took a sip, and didn't spit it out—boy, I can't tell you the satisfaction I felt. I'd actually done something for someone. I'd never realized before when I'd sat in a chair, taken a cookie, or filled my cup that someone had actually set up my chair, put that cookie into a basket, and prepared the brew I was drinking. It was funny and amazing how something so simple could be so satisfying." Warmed by this experience, Jack found himself actually eagerly looking forward to performing the second half of his sponsor's suggestions: going to a business meeting.

Jack shakes his head at the memory, and lets out a long, low whoosh of air. "When I said before it felt like a loss of innocence, I meant it. I couldn't believe the anger and the resentments and the vehemence and passion going on at this 'business meeting'! I was stunned for the first half hour of it. First of all, I hadn't realized how much I'd come to rely on the basic 'no cross talk' rule in Twelve Step meetings. That's what makes them so healing to me. In a regular AA meeting nobody barged in to 'fix' anybody else or give advice. We each had our moment in the sun, said what we had to say, and then it was the next person's turn. But that's not how this business meeting was. People actually had opinions about other people's opinions! There was *a lot* of trying to fix everybody else, or desperately trying to prove they were right and you were wrong—all stuff these people would never have dreamed of doing in a regular meeting! People I'd loved listening to in the rooms, men and women who were so calm and wise and sweet and tolerant—*whoa* boy, could they be the same people now? Like, when the treasurer read his report, three people raised their hands wildly to comment on this or that little detail in it, what *were* we doing with the money anyway, was enough going for literature or to Intergroup or for hospitality? Weren't we being charged too much rent? 'Excuse me, I didn't hear the fourth of the seven figures you read out ten minutes ago—would you repeat the whole list?' 'Hey, wait a minute, the report of our last meeting isn't complete—don't you remember we talked about setting up an anniversary party?' 'No we didn't—that was after the meeting was over; it wasn't *officially* part of it. . . .'" Jack is breathless. "Everyone seemed to want to adhere strictly to Robert's Rules of Order, but nobody seemed to know exactly what they were, so there was endless bickering about the protocol of making a motion and seconding it and whether this was the time for discussion or a vote and . . ."

His brow furrowed, Jack lets out a big sigh. "It seemed everyone had turned into a lunatic! At first I felt superior. Just sat there smugly, tsk-tsking at all these recovering alcoholics who didn't seem to be recovering anymore. I told myself I'd just sit and observe this peculiar phenomenon. I wouldn't sink to the level of actually *participating* in any of this terrible, backbiting nonsense. But then some new business came up and someone said something about possibly changing the format of my favorite Friday night meeting, the one I now made coffee at. . . . Well, you never saw anything like it. I exploded; there was no holding me back. How dare they tamper with something as wonderful as this meeting? Didn't they realize how we'd all come to depend on it being exactly the way it was, what a grievous wrong it would be to change even one tiny detail of it? I was so red in the face, so angry, that people actually quieted down and stared at me. Finally, a friend of mine reached for my hand and held it, trying to calm me down. 'Hey, man,' he whispered. 'Easy does it.' And suddenly it was like I came to. I saw what a maniac I'd turned into. I wasn't any better at business meetings than anyone else was! It was like my worst character defects had erupted. Rage, resentment, a feeling of superiority, even *hate*—all this terrible *anger!* I was really humbled by it. I apologized. The secretary told me it was okay, business meetings were difficult stuff, it was hard to hold on to our emotions. 'We're all recovering alcoholics,' he said. 'This is just one more part of grappling with recovery.'"

Jack catches his breath for a moment and calms down. "I should say that not all business meetings are as loud and unruly and difficult as this one was. I've had the courage to go back to a few, and I see now that maybe I'd just hit one when everyone seemed to be especially hungry, angry, lonely, or tired—that good old acronym HALT. Some business meetings are brief and peaceful and everyone's a model of good behavior. Some get out of hand. But it was an awakening to see how 'unsober' we could all be—especially *I* could be—as we tried to work on cooperating with one another outside the context of a regular AA meeting. It made me appreciate how involved all this stuff is, how unpredictable and complex people are. Like my sponsor says, 'This is a simple program for complicated people.' We have all kinds of traits. We're *human:* maybe that's the biggest shock. And human beings' personalities aren't always consistent; they run all over the place. Learning tolerance isn't always easy. Sometimes you have to go through a lot of anger and pain to come out the other side and realize that, hey, you're still sober and things will be okay if you just don't drink. But, boy, nobody told me what a lion's den even a group of recovering people can be! I have a huge respect for how complicated we are. And a huge respect for the power of Twelve Step programs to *meet* our complications, every one of them, with the kind of simplicity and grace I experience at the best meetings. This is amazing stuff."

Jack laughs again. "I'll never forget the look in my sponsor's eyes when I met him the day after that first business meeting. 'Had a good time?' he asked. His face was lit up, full of hilarity and more wisdom than I especially wanted to give him credit for at that moment. What I really wanted to do was kick him in the shins. Or maybe give him a hug. I'm still not sure which . . ."

When Somebody Asks YOU to Be a Sponsor

Jack gives us an overview of feelings, thoughts, and experiences many other recovering people go through when they participate in "service." A main conclusion of the second-year recoverers I've spoken to is that it's always more illuminating than you ever expect it will be.

"Sometimes I think AA and NA give me the best laboratory for learning what it means to be human," says Marya, a woman who works for a small party-catering service in a New Jersey town. "I used to think bartenders—and then caterers like me who get to watch whole groups of people get drunk at parties and make fools of themselves—got the best view of the human condition. But now I think you get that view best in the rooms. In the rooms we see one another *conscious.* However angry or bored or happy or depressed or excited we are, we're sober. We're seeing the real stuff. We're not seeing the result of some outside chemical 'help.' It's not only that we can't seem to avoid being who we really are, but we end up *remembering* it, and learning from it. No blackout erases our lessons. We're stuck with seeing ourselves day after day, being human. But I guess when it really hit me I was human was when somebody came up to me and asked me to be her sponsor. I've never felt more frail and inadequate and incompetent and just plain scared than I did at that moment."

Marya says that she'd made a private pact with herself not to sponsor anyone until she'd had three, maybe four, or even five years of sobriety. "I'm a slow learner about Twelve Step stuff," she says. "I'm still struggling with the implications of the First Step, and only sometimes do I feel I can 'surrender' to the Second and Third Steps. The rest of the Steps look to me like some distant mountain range. I have a feeling I'll get there someday, but not anytime soon. But the basic anxiety I had when Andrea came up to ask me to be her sponsor was, 'I don't know any more about this stuff than you do! How could I possibly help you?' I was also scared of the responsibility. Having to be there for someone every day. Be nice and helpful and understanding and—I don't know, I suppose I had some idea that a sponsor had to be a perfect parent and teacher and psychologist and spiritual guru. It was all I could do to get through my own life sober, one day at a time. How could I possibly be there for anyone else?" Marya pauses for a moment. "But there were other considerations too. I was scared of Andrea. She seemed, in a way, more powerful than I was. . . ."

Marya, at the age of forty-six, had just started to come out as a lesbian, "after twenty years of marriage and fifteen years of motherhood. I had always been aware of my feelings for women, but it's only been in sobriety—and very *early* sobriety, after all; I've only got eighteen months!—that I've begun to have the courage to explore these feelings, talk about them with other people. My husband and I went through a very messy divorce when I was still drinking, and he's got custody of our two kids, which I fought tooth and nail. Frankly, I'm still miserable about it; I go through a lot of guilt and anger that I'm not with them. But, to be truthful, it may be good that I've got time to myself. I feel awfully fragile right now. And while I hate to think of myself as selfishly going off to 'find myself,' I suppose that's what I need to do. I need time to figure out who I am, what I want my life to be, as well as just plain see what it's like to live life sober. Anyway, I've gone to some lesbian and gay meetings, joined some feminist groups, begun talking to other gay women. It's all very tentative and new for me, but I know I'm in the right territory. Andrea, however, is twenty years younger than me, has had a half dozen women lovers, is a committed political activist, totally out about being gay—a real force of nature. And she wanted *me* to her sponsor?"

At first Marya told Andrea that she didn't think she could say yes. "But Andrea looked so crestfallen. I knew how hard it was for me to ask someone to be my sponsor, and how crushing it is to be told no. And one thing I do hear in the rooms is, when you're asked to do service in AA, think very carefully before you say no. Andrea, who'd always seemed so strong and together and everything I couldn't be—including young!—suddenly looked so hurt and defenseless. So I changed my mind. I said, 'Okay, let's try it. But please, if you're disappointed in me, I won't be hurt if you decide to change sponsors, find someone else.' Secretly I was hoping that's exactly what would happen. . . ."

It did help Marya to talk about all this with her own sponsor. "My sponsor is a really sweet person. She's so different from Andrea, and in some ways from me. She's not gay, for one thing; she's about sixty-five years old, for another; and she just has this wonderful, patient, unconditional way of accepting me and loving me that, right now, I don't think I could do without. She always helps to give me perspective. She reminded me that all a sponsor is is another recovering alcoholic. And all that's required of a sponsor and sponsee is making contact. Somebody talks, somebody listens. That's it. Twelve Step programs are really simple. They're fellowships of people who are there to talk to and help one another, that's all."

When Marya could accept that all she had to do was answer the phone and *listen* when Andrea called, she began to relax a little. "I was feeling a kind of anxiety I think a lot of recovering addicts and alcoholics feel when someone reaches out for help. It's like I think I have to move in with anyone in trouble! Help them pay their rent, argue on their behalf with their mothers and bosses and lovers and spouses, baby-sit their kids, find them new jobs and homes, say exactly the right thing at exactly the right time—*forever*. With those kinds of expectations, it's no wonder I was scared stiff of sponsoring anyone. It's hard enough for me to have friends! I mean, I go to meetings and I've got my catering job; when everything is pretty much clearly mapped out, I can deal with it. When I know what the rules are, I feel okay, safe. But now that I'm coming out as a lesbian, and now that I've got this lesbian feminist activist young woman as a sponsee, the predictability of my life has received a major jolt. I feel, sometimes, like I'm out on a very precarious limb, with no net underneath me. . . ."

Marya didn't feel too much better about sponsoring Andrea after the first few calls. "It was awkward," Marya said. "I tried to calm down and listen and not jump in with unasked-for advice. I tried to 'identify, not compare.' But Andrea was talking to me about such foreign and intimidating stuff. How her lover was still smoking pot and putting a lot of sexual demands on Andrea, being jealous of the time Andrea spent at meetings and with her recovering friends, how Andrea decided to go to an Al-Anon meeting but couldn't stand the one she went to because everyone was straight and sexist and she got so furious she almost went to a bar to get blasted. How she was exasperated with most of the 'movement' women she knew because they just didn't seem committed enough to the cause, not like she felt. . . ." Marya shudders. "I was out of my depth. All I could do was listen. I couldn't imagine how to help Andrea with any of this! For one thing, she was so much more advanced about accepting her sexuality than I felt—I mean, I've never even had a female lover! What could I possibly say or do to help her?"

But then, Andrea shyly ended the sixth or seventh phone conversation with what seemed to Marya an extraordinary comment. "I always feel so much better when I talk to you," she said to Marya. "You give me such a feeling of peace." Marya was stunned: "I'd barely *said* anything to her all this time! I didn't feel like I'd done anything at all for her." But when she told her own sponsor about it, Marya says, "My sponsor laughed. She said she wanted to let me in on a secret. 'Do you know, sometimes when you call and you're all frazzled and distraught and full of anxiety, what I'm doing on the other end of the line is knitting. Sometimes, dear, I don't even especially listen to what you're telling me. Don't be shocked—I mean, my inner ear hears it all. But I can't count the times I've never said more than 'Mmm' or 'Really?' or 'Oh, that's terrible' in our entire conversation. Which is absolutely fine. Because I know you just need to make contact. My role isn't to give you advice, especially. My role is simply to be there. Sometimes that's all you've got to do: just be there. And that's what you're doing for Andrea right now. That's all she needs at the moment. You're doing just fine.'"

It's a bit misleading to suggest, as Marya's story may, that becoming a sponsor is a pressing concern for everyone in their second year of sobriety. From my observations, many recovering addicts and alcoholics don't actually end up sponsoring anyone until after their second year—sometimes well after. But the question "How could I possibly be anyone's sponsor?" begins to nag at many people I've talked to in their second year, even if they don't end up sponsoring anyone right away. And beneath that question is a central self-doubt: "What could *I* possibly have to give anyone else?"

One young man, Bob, acknowledges feeling this self-doubt particularly acutely. "I'm only twenty-three," Bob says. "I can't tell you how much I wonder, sometimes, if I even really *am* an addict, I mean, so many other people I meet in AA are in their thirties, forties, fifties, sixties—sometimes they don't even come into the program until they're twenty or thirty years older than I am! They've got decades of drinking and drugging experience. Horrendous stories. I mean, I went through some rough stuff, real blackout drinking and drugging in college. God knows I felt despair. But I didn't hit the kind of 'low bottom' I often hear about in the rooms. And sometimes I start to doubt myself, my motivations for being here. Am I just trying to find a girl-friend? Sometimes I think so. Am I looking for some mind-ex-pansion thing, some kind of group therapy that I could find a better version of elsewhere? Sometimes I think that too. Most times, when I allow myself to really identify with the feelings I hear other people express, these doubts disappear and I know I'm in exactly the right place, and that I deserve to be here. And I am starting to gravitate to men and women closer to my age, and lis-ten very carefully to why *they* say they're here. But the idea of sponsoring anyone else? Gotta draw the line there. I don't know anything yet. I'm a *kid.*" Bob smiles a little. "Of course when I go on in this self-denigrating way to my sponsor, he reminds me that I *have* managed to stay sober for a year and a half. And he re-minds me of so many people I've seen in the rooms, even in the space of time I've been going to meetings, who can't seem ever to get ninety days together. Ten days and they're out. Maybe fif-teen days. But they can't seem to sustain it. In and out, in and out. He says this doesn't mean I'm better than they are, but I do have some experience, strength, and hope they don't have yet. Which means maybe I *do* know something after all."

Because sobriety is such an individual experience, because each of us brings such different "baggage" into it—age, back-ground, education, solvency, likes and dislikes, different degrees and types of illness and health—the feeling of separateness we've been exploring as an overriding theme throughout this book is always waiting to rear up and make us feel isolated again. That old voice tells us once more that we're not really like anyone else in AA or NA, points out the foolishness of thinking we could ever have anything significant to share with anyone else in the program. But when, as Bob was persuaded to do, we take a mo-ment to look at a few simple facts, like the fact that we've man-aged to keep from picking up a drink or a drug for over a year, we may begin to feel a kind of basic commonality with other people who are managing to do the same thing. We can see what we're doing as a genuine gift and triumph. Sustaining that gift and triumph is, we see, teaching us something valuable, something that we *can* pass on to others who express the desire to hear about it.

Of course, the self-doubt keeps coming back. Bob says, "I know I need to keep reconnecting with my sponsor and with my friends at meetings every day. Otherwise I'm like a balloon floating away, the string unattached to anything down here on earth. Service, even if I can't yet imagine sponsoring anyone else, is a good way of reminding me where the earth is. I've become the treasurer for my home group meeting. I'm the guy who says, 'We have no dues or fees, but we do have expenses. . . .' I can't tell you how much just getting up in front of a group of people, rattling off my spiel, then passing the basket, then counting the money and keeping track of it, has done for my self-esteem. It's something that goes so far beyond whatever usefulness I may have as a treasurer. I've been given a specific role to play, beyond the central one I've always had of simply sitting in a meeting and sharing. I know that is doing service too. Just by going to meetings, my sponsor reminds me, we're 'powers of example,' and we're helping others. But actually getting up there and doing my 'no dues or fees' thing feels good. It's become part of what keeps me coming back, no matter what my doubts may be about being too young or not having hit a low enough bottom."

For so many second-year recoverers, "service" does seem to have a kind of magical quality; it can deliver so much more than you ever expect it to. But sometimes, a number of people in their second year tell me, the rewards of service can turn into a burden. When we turn to service with desperation or unrealistic expectations, it can backfire. Witness Dan.

Overdoing It

Like Jack, Dan is used to running things. But unlike Jack, who in his role as advertising executive ran things in a very visible way—playing the boss, pulling rank, showing off—Dan had learned to pull strings from behind the scenes. "I guess the bald truth is," Dan admits, "I'm an undercover control freak."

Dan, a thirty-year-old legal assistant, says he always identifies strongly with anybody he hears talk about low self-esteem. "I mean, look at my job," he says. "I'm a legal assistant, not a lawyer. I never believed I had the stuff to actually go through law school and get hired as an attorney by anybody. But I'll work like hell for somebody else. People tell me I know more than most lawyers do, and that I end up doing most of my bosses' work. But it doesn't really register. My bosses—I work for about six lawyers—have something I don't have. Guts."

Dan comes from an alcoholic family, "but not an out-in-the-open, drunken-father-beating-you-up kind of family. My dad drank after work in a bar and he always got home late, after I was asleep. He didn't throw any tantrums, wreck the house, or hit anybody. He just was never there." Dan says he grew up with a kind of Napoleon complex: "I'm short and I tend to be over-weight. Kids at school used to joke that I'd be great at bowling— as the ball. I was the guy everybody picked on. I've been in therapy about it. It's hard for me to admit some of this stuff. Like being chased by neighborhood kids, hiding under cars so they couldn't get at me to beat me up. Taking long, drawn-out, out-of-the-way walks back from the library so I wouldn't run into this or that bully. I can face a little of it now, but it's still hard. I mean, I still have this image of myself as a short, fat, ugly coward. All that stuff that happened in childhood still hurts."

Escaping into drugs and booze was something Dan learned to do when he went to college. "I went to this big factory of a state university in the Midwest. Thousands of people. You were a number more than a person, which was fine with me. It was the first place I ever was that people didn't make fun of me, pick on me, give me a hard time. Mostly they ignored me."

They did, anyway, until Dan discovered two things: the inhibition-releasing powers of marijuana and beer, and the fact that he seemed to be a born organizer. "Everyone smoked dope and drank beer in my dormitory; it was just something you did if you went to college. So I did too. And, oh, the relief! I can still remember now what it felt like that first time. It was like a huge weight had been taken off my head, my back. I was able to laugh. I wasn't so scared of everybody. I could tell a few jokes. It was like pot and alcohol released the human being in me. I almost felt *normal*. And I also discovered that I was good at stuff. I mean, someone on my dorm floor said hey, wouldn't it be neat to have a big party with the girl's dorm next to us, and, whacked out on pot, I started to work it all out on the spot. Figured out how many kegs to get, came up with ideas for a real toga party— it all came out of that movie *Animal House*, I guess, but nobody seemed to notice—started getting people to agree to bring potato chips, or clear out the rec hall we had in the dorm basement, come up with decorations, decide on the music. I was taking charge! I'd never done anything like this before; it was heady stuff. Somehow, though, it wasn't like I was trying to draw attention to myself. That is, I didn't want to be made president of anything, or do anything high-profile. I just wanted to be liked. That was it. And be thought of as indispensable . . ."

Making himself "indispensable" was something Dan got good at doing. "I was the stage manager of the drama club, the guy who organized parties for the football team, the guy in any group you could count on to raise his hand when somebody asked, 'Could anybody volunteer to . . .?' I was doing lousy work at school, slid by with about a C+ average, but that didn't bother me. I was a part of people's *lives* doing what I was doing, running everything quietly, saying yes to everybody, figuring out ways to make things work. And as long as there was more beer and more reefer, which there always was, I could keep up the social end of things too. It became essential to be everybody's reliable friend— the guy you could 'always count on.' It was the only way I could imagine being liked, and accepted."

Over ten years have passed since Dan discovered what he felt was his "calling" as everybody's helping hand, doormat, secretary, and party organizer. "I actually cried when I left college," Dan says, "because I'd worked so hard to make it in this environment, and I'd finally found people and a place that I understood, that I could get to accept me. I knew the ropes someplace—the first time in my life I'd ever felt that. But when I had to leave, I panicked. What was I going to do? How could I find another environment as safe and understandable, as workable, as the one I'd had in college?"

At first, Dan managed to get in with a bunch of guys who were renting a big apartment in a run-down section of a nearby city. Dan was hoping it would be a continuation of college. He could manage these guys' lives the way he ran everything in college, couldn't he? But it didn't turn out that way.

"It was humiliating," Dan says. "There were seven of us: six of them and one of me. It turned out three of the guys actively didn't want me to be part of the group; the other three had only said yes because the more there were of us, the less rent anybody would have to pay. But they weren't real friends—they were just guys I sort of knew from school. I really felt left out. They'd go out to a game or a concert or a bar and not tell me. It was like my childhood all over again. I was the odd man out once again." What Dan did on his frequent nights alone was drink and smoke dope. "I could put away cases of beer, and I was in this constant haze of dope. I just got fatter and stupider—at least I see that now, but then I was just trying to escape, trying not to feel anything. It was obvious I couldn't fit in anywhere, so why try? College had been a fluke, nothing like that would ever happen again."

To support his beer and pot habit and to pay his small rent, Dan did temporary jobs: "I'd do some typing or filing for a few days, make a little money, then veg out again on beer and pot. That was my life." As if by reflex, Dan was a good worker; even when he was hung over, as he frequently was, he couldn't seem to help being efficient, quick, and organized. As a result of his good performance, his boss at one temp job offered him a full-time assistant position—the one he still basically has today. "By this time living with six other guys who obviously couldn't stand me was becoming intolerable, even when I was smashed and stoned. At least now I'd have the money to get myself into my own place. So I accepted the offer and moved into a small rat-hole apartment."

Describing the next years of his life as simple, Dan says, "I was the best little boy in the world during the day, and got blasted out of my mind at night. My only contact with human beings was at work. I discovered another place I could make myself indispensable, and I did. I was everybody's errand boy, typist, coffee-getter, and, as I learned more about the law from the letters I had to type and file, everybody's researcher and proofreader and, well, you name it, I became it. But when I left the job every day, it was like turning out a light. I went home and drank and smoked dope, and completely blanked out. An alarm clock got me up the next morning, and however bad I felt—and, oh Lord! sometimes the hangovers were *incredible*—I dragged myself back to work to continue being indispensable."

Dan came into AA and NA not because of any dramatic, illuminating revelation or terrible bottom that was significantly worse than what he was going through already. "It happened like this," he says. "One day, as I was taking the bus to work in the morning and I looked up at a poster advertising a drug and alcohol hot line, I started to cry. Simple as that. It was like an involuntary reflex. I wasn't even aware that strongly of any emotion, except, maybe, the huge, hungry desire I've always felt in the center of me for release. But they had this picture on the poster of a nice-looking, calm woman leaning on a rake in her backyard, the most normal, nice person you could imagine, working in her garden just like any other normal, nice person, and a quote from her that read, 'Once I wanted to kill myself. Now I want to live.' And I started to cry. That was all, I just cried." It was the first time, Dan says, "that I actually allowed myself to feel my despair. The first time I realized how desperately unhappy I really was."

Dan called the hot line number and, through a therapist he eventually hooked up with, began going first to AA, then to NA meetings when he realized he wanted to deal more specifically with marijuana. "And it's been wonderful," Dan says. The openings we've explored throughout this book—the sense of connecting with other people, of allowing yourself to receive help—all of this has begun to happen for Dan. But one aspect of his personality hasn't changed at all. As Dan says, "I found a whole new arena to become indispensable in!"

After he had ninety days of sobriety in AA, then in NA, Dan began to feel his hand reflexively shoot up whenever anybody requested a volunteer. "At first I was setting up chairs, helping with the coffee, cleaning out ashtrays at the end of a meeting, taking out the garbage. Then, after six months, I became one group's secretary and the other group's treasurer. After a year, in addition to doing all the stuff I've just mentioned, I began to speak at meetings, both AA and NA, whenever I could. A couple of months ago, I got involved with helping out at the detox unit at our local hospital and in the men's prison AA and NA groups." Dan's life had turned into a unbelievable mesh of AA, NA, and his job at the law firm. "Strangely, though," Dan says, "with all of my sticking to the rules and doing everything I was supposed to and taking on every responsibility I could, I never got a sponsor, either in NA or AA. That only happened when I signed up to be somebody else's sponsor in the 'interim sponsor' book they've got at my AA group. As I was doing that, the chairman of that meeting asked me if I had a sponsor. Not that that would have excluded me from becoming a sponsor myself, but he said he was curious. I told him I didn't have one. I realized, in fact, that I'd always pushed away the idea of getting a sponsor, because I was scared. Having a sponsor meant two things to me: letting somebody *in*, which terrified me, and making myself vulnerable to somebody else's opinions and advice. I was damned if anyone else was going to tell me what to do! That was the real feeling. And it amazed me. I mean, here I'd gotten myself into this incredible mess of deadlines and saying yes to everybody. Wasn't I already doing whatever anyone else wanted me to?"

Dan says not having a sponsor began to rankle in him. It brought up a lot of uncomfortable issues, such as the fact that he'd never connected intimately with another human being in his life, or the fact that he might still be covering up his fear of people, his pain about feeling "different," his terror of being rejected, by losing himself in all his frantic activities. Maybe he needed to talk to someone about this, someone who could give him some perspective about what he was doing to himself in sobriety. The truth was, he was still as lonely now as he'd ever been. He'd never really "surrendered" to certain truths about his own nature. It took all the courage he had, but Dan decided to sign up in the sponsorship book not to become a sponsor, but to get one.

"I was hooked up the next week with the guy who's still my sponsor, John. John is a farmer. He works some land about forty miles outside the city I live in, and he comes in nearly every night for a meeting. He couldn't be more different from me. He's the calmest man I ever met. Sure, he works hard, but he doesn't get nuts about it. He just does what he has to do. He's got a wife and five kids, most of them grown, one still in high school. The point is, he's got a life full of other people who genuinely care about him and who he genuinely cares about. I realize that my only connection to people, even in sobriety, is based on making myself useful to them—but not in a truly giving way. It's the old bartending self I was when I drank: I'll give you this if you give me that. And the payoff for me was a kind of acceptance, any kind of 'sure, we'll let you stay, Dan, if you keep up the good work.' John offers me something so much simpler. I don't feel I have to be anybody special with him; I can just be myself. The only advice he's given me in the four months I've hooked up with him, apart from the eternal 'Don't drink, go to meetings,' is 'Slow down.' He hasn't gotten on my back about the activities I've thrown myself into. He doesn't get upset about it. He seems to know I needed to go through a period of frantic stuff, because that's who I've always been. But he lets me know that I've got options. And if I slow down, I'll begin to see what those options are."

Dan has made the decision to "cool it" with some aspects of service. "I'm discovering two things as a result. Even if I'm not the one who makes the coffee, the coffee gets made. Things get done even if I don't do them! But the other and maybe more important thing is, I'm still acceptable if I'm not trying to be who everyone wants me to be. I'm acceptable just because *I am*." Dan looks quizzically at the ceiling for a moment. "Could I be saying this?" He laughs. "This is all so new. It's still an uncomfortable thought that I might be okay just as I am. But John is helping me to see that maybe I can let up on myself a bit more each day, and see that I don't have to turn myself inside out to be accepted, to be loved."

Taking the Lessons of Service Outside the Rooms

So many second-year recovering people who have begun to do service in Twelve Step programs have told me that there's a kind of spillover from what they feel and do in the rooms to the rest of their lives. Jennifer gives a particularly moving example of this, one that seems to reflect a lot of other recovering people's experience.

"I used to hate family gatherings," Jennifer says. "In fact, I made the conscious decision to stay away from my family for the whole first year and a half of my sobriety. But now that I'm coming up on my two-year anniversary—now that I've proven to myself I can get through some difficult stuff sober—I find, quite spontaneously, that I *miss* my family. I want to see, at least briefly, how it might be to see them the way I am now."

Jennifer's family was not full of alcoholics; she does not feel she "inherited" the disease from her forebears. "This gave me a lot of trouble," Jennifer says. "I grew up with the message that our family didn't have the sorts of problems 'other people' did. We were brought up to stuff our feelings and stay in control. I was the middle child, and I guess a pretty classic example of one. My little sister got all the attention for being the baby; my older sister seemed to get all the privileges. I became the go-between, the peacemaker, the one who smoothed things over. But I hid a lot of resentment and anger. I never felt like anyone paid attention to me. My drinking started surreptitiously, as a rebellion, when I was a little girl, about eight or nine. My parents would give these dinner parties and I'd sneak in and drain everybody's glass after all the grown-ups left the living room to go to the dining room. It was mostly water, but I got a warm feeling from even the diluted alcohol. That warm feeling was so nice. It was the only time I felt cared for, really, feeling like I did after I drank somebody's leftover scotch and water. Later, when I was a teenager, I'd sneak scotch out of the liquor cabinet. Then when I was about sixteen I hung around older kids who were able to buy liquor, and we'd drink together almost every night, certainly every weekend. God, the mouthwash and breath mints I went through to hide the smell!"

Jennifer clung to the "warm feelings" alcohol gave her for years. "But by the time I was in my late twenties," she says, "it was no longer reliable. I couldn't always get to that feeling of safety. God—safety! It's a wonder I'm *alive*. I was starting to black out, which I'd never done when I was a kid. It was so unpredictable. Sometimes I'd be able to drink nearly a whole bottle of scotch and not feel especially high; other times two or three drinks would send me under. I mean *way* under. No idea where I was. Ending up in strange beds with stranger people. I was pretty classic, I guess, especially when it came to denial. I kept hearing this inner voice telling me I couldn't be an alcoholic, nobody in my family is an alcoholic, it's all a failure of my willpower. Or maybe I was just nuts. Yes, that appealed to me. I was somehow a bad seed, crazy, missed the boat. Something essential had been left out of me that had gotten into 'normal' people. I was as disabled as any person missing an arm or a leg, as anyone who was blind or deaf. Except I was worse, because what I was missing was *inside*. I could never get better, never get over whatever it was that made me crazy. It was like I was stained in some irrevocable way, and nothing could get the stain out."

But after one particularly frightening blackout—"I woke up in a bus going out to some suburb, headed for God knew where"—Jennifer decided to look for help. Like many recovering people, she began with therapy. "It never occurred to me I was an alcoholic, or that I could be. I was just trying to find out why I was so crazy." Her therapist turned out to have a great deal of experience working with alcoholics; she steered Jennifer to the rooms, and Jennifer took to AA with huge relief and an enormous faith that seemed to come out of nowhere. "I didn't realize how hungry I was for recovery," Jennifer says. "I'm one of the lucky ones. It's worked for me right off."

But now, after nearly two years of sobriety, Jennifer faced going back to her family. "It wasn't even a particularly big occasion," she says. "I'd somehow talked my way out of Christmas for the past two years—couldn't take that much time away from work, I said. I live about a thousand miles away from where my parents and most of my family live; it just wasn't feasible, I told them, to get out to see them. Too expensive and not enough time. So they were surprised when I said I wanted to go to my uncle's eightieth birthday party. To tell the truth, I didn't especially feel close to my uncle, my mother's older brother. He was a strange, distant man. He was a fairly prominent attorney in his day—had offices in Europe as well as the United States. I remember him as this great big commanding presence, sort of European, foreign, exotic, hard to approach and understand. Physically a big man: strong, larger than life. He dressed so beautifully, that was one thing I remember about him. In this old-fashioned way: He always wore a vest with a gold pocket watch. So different from the rest of my small-town family. Anyway, I'd heard he'd had a stroke a few years before, but I didn't take much notice of it. I was too drunk, for one thing. But none of this especially mattered to me now. I was really going back to find out what it would be like to see my sisters and my parents again. Would I freak out? Would I have the courage to tell them I was a recovering alcoholic? Or did I have to tell them at all? I was full of nervous energy, my brain buzzed, projecting any number of scenarios—me giving speeches about my recovery at the dining room table while everyone gasped in horror, that sort of thing. But nothing prepared me for what really happened. . . ."

Jennifer had arranged to get home on the day of her uncle's birthday party. Because of a slightly delayed plane, she got to her uncle's house after the festivities had already begun. "I was so scared," Jennifer says, "as I walked up the drive to the house. I knew my whole family was inside; it was like some terrible moment of truth had come, and every fiber in me was screaming, 'Run away! Get the hell out of here before it's too late!' Every horrible memory of their coldness, their neglect, their being nasty to me—it all came back. But I steeled myself to walk in anyway. I tried to remind myself that all I had to do was 'show up'—just like I hear in AA—and trust that God would take care of the rest."

Jennifer opened the door and walked into the living room, the party going in full swing. Her mother and father seemed genuinely happy to see her: "They actually ran up and hugged me!" Jennifer says disbelievingly. "And my sisters were nice too. It was all just fine. It was all just fine until I looked across the room and saw my uncle." Jennifer's uncle was almost literally a shadow of the man he had been. "He seemed so tiny, so frail. His daughter, my cousin, who my mother told me had devoted her whole life now to taking care of her father, was feeding him cake and ice cream with a spoon. He was blind and nearly deaf. He could barely speak." Jennifer closes her eyes for a moment. "You can't know what it was like for me. It wasn't that I was close to him at any time in my childhood. But he'd always been this huge, strong, exotic, mythical figure to me! And now—now, it was unbelievable. It was like some part of him, some major part of him, had already died. I couldn't take my eyes off him.

"But something was even worse than seeing him so frail and sick and weak. The only person who was paying him any real attention, the person who was treating him like a real human being, was his daughter. Everyone else near him was standing around stiffly, uncomfortably, as if they would have paid a lot of money to be anywhere but where they were. My cousins, friends of the family—you could cut the tension with a knife. I saw my cousin, my uncle's daughter, laughing and cooing and telling jokes and petting her father, but everyone else around them was dead silent, shifting from foot to foot, like they were all embarrassed to be witnessing what was going on between this barely alive father and his overzealous daughter."

It was then Jennifer experienced perhaps the biggest surprise of the day. "I don't understand what came over me," she says. "But suddenly it became important for me to go over to him, hold his hand, talk to him, treat him like a *person*. It's not like I turned into Mother Teresa or anything. I mean, I didn't feel especially noble. I just wanted to make contact with him. So I did. I joined my cousin, saw that in fact my uncle had not completely lost his mind or his hearing or his ability to speak, and started to have a conversation with him. Since he couldn't see me, I told him who I was, held his hand, and then fell into a stream of memories I didn't realize I had! I remembered how he'd taught me to dive when I was a little girl, off a float in a nearby lake—how afraid I'd been, and how patient he'd been with me. I remembered when a Chinese restaurant had opened in a nearby town and how my uncle was the only member of the family who'd had the courage to try it—we were all such Midwestern meat-and-potato cowards—and how it was because I knew he'd gone there that I was able to try Chinese food too. Now it was my favorite food! I told him I remembered his wonderful law office, all the dark wood and the leather volumes and the green glass lamps, and how special a place it had always seemed to me." Jennifer pauses and sighs.

"You have to understand, this wasn't a favorite uncle or anything. I really hadn't thought much about him, hadn't seen him as a particularly important or influential person in my childhood. But I had this fund of wonderful memories I found I could call on nonetheless. And I can't describe his reaction. He was so frail—he had incomplete control over his facial muscles, from the paralysis he'd suffered from his stroke, so it was hard for him even to smile. But he could still talk. And he spoke, slowly, but distinctly enough to capture the kind of vaguely intimidating British accent I remembered he had when he was at his peak. Anyway, he said, 'Thank you for reminding me of the happiness of my life. It has been all the more marvelous because of your presence.' It was my uncle as I remember him: the same old-fashioned way of saying things, the politeness. It was wonderful; I can't tell you how much it meant to me. And for the rest of the party his daughter and I stayed with him. He actually managed to get up out of his wheelchair and, with our help and the help of the cane, hobbled a few steps around the living room. As he did so, we introduced him to members of the family who happened to be standing nearby. We managed to draw them into some conversations—to involve them in a way they hadn't been involved before. It was extraordinary. But never more so than when, after he was tired and back in his chair and dozing from his exertions, my cousin looked at me with tears in her eyes and thanked me. 'You gave him so much,' she said. And I was amazed. Because a part of me realized she was right, and I could acknowledge it.

"But the source of being able to give to my uncle—boy, it sure wasn't just from me. I knew that with my whole heart and soul. The strength I'd unexpectedly found in myself came from somewhere outside me. I don't like going on about 'Higher Power' too much. I hated church when I was a kid, and I'm very uncomfortable with even the word 'God.' But somehow, some kind of larger force was working through me. That's all I know. And I'd learned everything I know about that force through AA. All the time I'd spent at meetings, listening, sharing, sometimes making coffee or cleaning up after a meeting—all the time I'd spent doing 'service'—all of that was starting to pay off in some peculiar ways right now. It had simply taught me to be *present* in a way I'd never been before."

This feeling of being present stayed with Jennifer throughout the rest of her family visit. "It's not that my family didn't annoy me in some of the old ways," she says. "Believe me, they did. My father still had his pompous opinions about everything. My mother still bickered at him endlessly. My sisters were completely absorbed in their own lives; nobody really seemed to care about the details of my life. But, strangely, it didn't matter as much. It's like I'd learned not to take the bait and fall into the old resentments. I was simply *calmer* than I can ever remember being with them. And by the end of the weekend, they'd noticed. 'You're different,' my older sister said. 'I feel like I've got to get to know you all over again.' My mother and father actually were affectionate with me when I left; something was different between us. More love had been allowed to come out, I guess. But the source of all this, or at least the source of my part in all this—I can only pin it to what I've learned in sobriety through AA."

Jennifer says she thinks of her uncle often, and especially remembers how freeing was the feeling of connection she felt toward him. "How strange it is that I feel the most freedom when I'm actually in there pitching, doing something. When I'm taking on the responsibility of reaching out. When I drank, my idea of freedom was to flee from responsibility, from having to do anything at all. And now, in sobriety, I'm learning that 'showing up' is what leads to freedom, not running away."

But part of the inner freedom she feels when she thinks about her uncle also comes from what she says is her "strong identification with him. When I walked in and saw that nobody was paying him any real attention, that here was this human being who, although ostensibly the *reason* for the party, was being next to completely ignored—well, I knew how he felt. It's as simple as that. And I realized from having listened to so many alcoholics in so many AA meetings that his feeling of being misunderstood and neglected, this terrible feeling of being alone, is something we've *all* felt. The only way out is to *make a connection.* Reach out for help, and reach out to someone who needs help and is asking for it. Sobriety doesn't only happen in an AA meeting. We've got opportunities to make these kinds of connections everywhere. At work, with friends, family, strangers you bump into in the street—everywhere. That's the revelation. I can take this act on the road and even take it back home to my family! And, believe me, if I can make sobriety work when I go home to my folks, I can make it work anywhere."

Again we return to an ongoing theme throughout this exploration of second-year sobriety: moving from feeling separate to feeling connected. In the final section of this book, we'll turn the prism another degree or two to see how this feeling of connection to the outside world can be bolstered by experience that happens inside, in a way that many recovering alcoholics and addicts label "spiritual."

The very word *spiritual* can be problem for a lot of recovering people. When we hear in Twelve Step meetings that all recovery is at root spiritual, some of us feel ourselves resisting. Flashes of overbearing nuns, rabbis, ministers; teachers or parents who threatened us with various versions of "hell" if we didn't "behave"; any number of personal, negative feelings can crop up in this spiritual arena. Like Jennifer, a number of recovering people are able to clue into what they call "faith in a Higher Power" without any trouble. We don't all resist in the same ways. But in the second year of sobriety, with more than a year of experience dealing with the outer world sober, most of us start to take a new look at what might be inside, what might actually be *fueling* our ongoing ability to stay sober.

Let's take a look at some second-year findings about spirituality. As with so much else in sobriety, expect some surprises. The effect of spirituality on day-to-day life is almost always different from what you predict it will be—or so say the variety of second-year recoverers you'll meet next.

five

A Second-Year Take on Spirituality

"What's the biggest change I've experienced in sobriety?" Matthew concentrates, choosing his words carefully. "Vocabulary," he finally says. "Sobriety, to me, has been a matter of changing vocabulary. Words that used to make me want to run out of the room, words like *faith, God, humility, surrender,* and *powerlessness,* now just don't have the same meaning anymore. I don't bolt when I hear them. Now I even get some comfort from them. You're looking for a complete change, you got one right there."

Matthew says he supposes he's always been an intellectual, "if you mean by that somebody who reads everything, thinks a lot, and can talk like he went to college. The only 'value' I think I got from my parents, who were otherwise pretty much total washouts was that it was a good idea to go to school. What they had in mind was, it's a good idea to go to school and learn to do something that could get you a lot of money and prestige, like become a doctor or lawyer. Luckily, I was on a scholarship; I went to college and studied philosophy, literature, and art. If they'd had to pay for any of it, I'd have been cut off cold. As it was, I was cut off from them emotionally. If there were any two people who were completely unprepared to have kids, it was my

parents. They loathed each other, for one thing. Simple arith-
metic reveals that my mother married my father because she
'had' to: I was born six months after their marriage. I did not
grow up in what anyone could call a happy home."

Matthew's father was, he said, a closet alcoholic. "We were
Jewish, not that we were observant or anything; I never even had
a bar mitzvah, but I was still told we were Jewish, and therefore
different from other people. And I grew up with the very strong
message that Jews weren't alcoholics; it just wasn't possible.
However, my father had his private stash of sweet wine that he
drank when he got off work, and all day Saturday and Sunday,
and frankly the man went through most of his life blitzed. There
was complete denial about it. He was always 'taking it'—never
drinking it—because it 'calmed the stomach.' If that's what he
was taking it for, it didn't seem to work very well. At least, I've
never met a man more full of pent-up fury than my father. After
a certain amount of his 'medicine,' he'd just get nasty and snide
and sometimes even violent. Sometimes he'd even take a swing
at my mother; she'd lock herself in the bedroom. Then it was my
turn; I was like an open target. Maybe I was a masochist, but I
never locked myself away when he went on a tirade. I just stood
there and took it. When I was older, I started talking back to him.
He wanted a fight? I was ready to fight. I hated the man, if you
want to know the truth. Years later, after a good fifteen years of
no contact with him, I heard from a cousin that he died of a heart
attack in the middle of the street, walking home from the liquor
store. My mother had died a few years before that; I didn't go to
her funeral and I didn't go to my father's. By that time I was living in a small hotel room, chugging vodka. I'd become as drunk
and nasty and self-hating as my dad had ever been. But we'd dis-
owned each other completely."

What Matthew did while he chugged vodka in his small hotel
room was read—"until the words got too blurry to make out"—
an enormous range and number of "philosophical, theological,

and spiritual tomes. For some reason, the whole idea of spirituality had always fascinated me. I guess it was because my life was so rotten, I had felt so much pain and self-loathing, I couldn't imagine what the *purpose* of any of it could be. I'd started drinking in college—took to it like the born drunk I am—and I started a search for a different kind of spirit at the same time. In fact, 'Alcohol and the Search for Meaning' was the title of a big paper I did for a literature class. I took three of the biggest drunks in American literature, Fitzgerald, Faulkner, and O'Neill, and proceeded to go through their works, labeling stuff they only wrote because they were drunks. I had a kind of second sight about this stuff. Intuitively, I knew what a drunk was attracted to, what he couldn't help thinking and writing about. The funny thing was, one of the greatest quotes I found as I researched backup material about alcoholism was from the psychologist Carl Jung in a letter he'd written to the cofounder of AA, Bill Wilson! Talk about setting the stage for my future recovery. I was a Jung freak anyway: I loved all that stuff about archetypes and the collective unconscious and the hero's journey; it really appealed to my grandiose ideas of myself as a misunderstood heroic genius. Anyway, I can still remember the quote I used from Jung: 'You see,' he'd written to Bill Wilson, 'alcohol in Latin is *spiritus* and you use the same word for the highest religious experience as well as for the most depraving poison.' Yes, that was exactly it, I thought. In essence, drinking covered up a profound spiritual quest—maybe, in fact, it *was* a profound spiritual quest itself! Naturally I was a drunk! What better, more profound thing was there to be? Some people, in fact the greatest artists and writers, were so exquisitely sensitive and attuned to the world that they'd go crazy if they couldn't escape through booze. Alcohol to them—and to me, too—was as essential to their development and well-being as water and air were to the rest of humanity. I had it all neatly tied up. When I tied one on, I was getting closer to the Truth. It was as much a blessing as a curse to be a drunk.

We were the real chosen people. We could see beyond and beneath, as long as we kept drinking. So what if we were killing ourselves? What was death next to all this Truth?"

Matthew managed, after college, to hook into a civil service post-office job: "Mindless desk work from which I could virtually never be fired, and which gave me just enough money to cover my hotel room and the cost of booze. It was the late sixties when I got out of college, but I never did much pot or acid. Smoked some weed a couple of times, didn't like the sort of spooky otherworld feelings it gave me. I felt out-of-the-world enough already. Did an acid trip once with a girl I met in a bar; it made me think we'd turned into huge cockroaches—actually, I was the cockroach, and she'd turned into a rat who *ate* cockroaches. As crazy as I was and am, I draw the line at moving into a Kafka novel. No, booze was it for me. It did what I wanted it to. It gave me an out. My father turned out to be right. It did 'calm the stomach,' at least for a while. It also calmed the brain, to the point of catatonia maybe, but it worked. It got me out of the world. And who wanted to be in the world?"

Matthew somehow kept up his job, and through the next twenty years found his reading interests move steadily toward the occult: "Way out stuff, spiritual Eastern-type guru literature, weird diets, the tarot, mantras, hybrids of the *I Ching* and the Kabbalah. I'd get drunk and sort of do a mind-journey; at least that's what I told myself, desperately trying to get some kind of answer for why I was alive, why I had to put up with the boring misery of my life. Suicide seemed a logical solution more than once. But for some reason, I never tried to kill myself—other than how I was doing it already, with booze. Just went to work; then sometimes—although not often toward the end—I'd go to a bar, mostly to see if I could get a woman to go to bed with me, then go home, usually alone, to my messy little hotel room, read something 'profound,' and drink myself into oblivion. I was a physical mess. I stank, I was bloated, felt like I was on the edge of death, but nothing could put me out for good. I kept waking up in the morning and doing it again and again."

Matthew says he eventually stopped drinking not because he wanted to, but because he got caught at work. "By the last two or three years of my drinking, I was bringing in flasks or pint bottles of vodka to chug in the men's room. Usually I hid myself in a stall, but one morning all the stalls were being used, so I took a chance and drank out of a pint bottle right out in the open, in front of the sinks. My supervisor took that moment to walk into the men's room. I didn't know what to do, really, so I smiled at him and said, 'Want some?' He was not amused. Although I was so locked in to my job that there was no real question of firing me, he said he could transfer me to another department and make my life a lot more miserable—and he would definitely do that if I didn't stop getting drunk at work. Apparently I hadn't been so cool about hiding it, after all. He said he'd been getting reports from my co-workers for the past year that I'd seemed blasted out of my mind. He wasn't going to let me besmirch his department. Actually, he wasn't a monster about it. He told me it would be all right with him if I took some time off, went to a rehab, got some help. I was about to tell him to take this job and stuff it until he said that. I thought, boy, it might be nice to be locked up somewhere and totally taken care of. I could run on at the mouth at group therapy sessions or whatever, share all of my profound spiritual insights, and, who knows, maybe it might not be so bad to dry out for a while either. I said, okay, I'd shape up if I could ship out for a bit. The idea of time off in a padded room was sort of appealing."

Matthew did in fact go to rehab. At first he resisted the Twelve Step approach they tried to make him take. "Sounded like a lot of quasi-Christian *mea culpa* stuff to me. How we had to find out what part *we* had taken in the messes our lives had become—all that stuff sounded like they wanted me to say it was my fault I'd had the lousy hand of cards their 'Higher Power' had dealt me. I was damned if I was going to fall for that line." But Matthew had one extraordinary experience that had nothing to do with the language the rehab counselors were using.

"I was prepared to argue with everybody,"Matthew said. "That's what I'd grown up doing, and what I'd become very good at doing. What I wasn't prepared for was what happened at the end of the first AA meeting in rehab. We all got up and held hands. A woman was on my right and a man on my left. I was aware of nothing at that moment except that people were actually touching me. The feel of warm human flesh, in a way that wasn't sexual—I couldn't remember ever having experienced that before! Simple contact between people. It was extraordinary. In fact, it shut me up. For the rest of that day and evening, I was quiet. I wasn't rushing in to show how stupid the Twelve Steps were, or how much smarter I was than anybody else. I was aware of nothing except how it felt to press my hand against somebody's else's hand. And it moved me to remember it. I felt like crying. When had I ever cried in my life? I couldn't remember. But something got to me."

Whatever it was that got to Matthew, he claims it's become the source of his having been able to stop drinking and stay stopped for nearly two years now. And in that time, he says, "I've learned a whole new way of listening and thinking, a way that doesn't have so much to do with that intellectual analysis I tried my whole life to bring to everything. There's a way of listening with your heart in which argument has no place. The whole urge for combat I had, though sometimes it pops up now too, of course, is slowly being replaced by something else. A new kind of softening or receptivity, I guess. It's very different. And, as I said when I started, one of the biggest net results is that my very understanding of *words* has changed. Humility no longer means what I thought it meant: humiliation. Powerlessness and surrender don't mean that I'm a weak-willed wimp, a loathsome little worm. Accepting what I'm powerless over gives me clarity;

it's not an announcement that I'm constitutionally inadequate. And I don't have to run away from the word *God* anymore either. Not that I've got any better definition of God than I ever did messing around in theology or the occult—I don't. But the word and the concept of God no longer fill me with such urgency, dread, or frustration. Some see change has happened, just from not drinking and going to AA meetings, just like they told me it would. I don't understand it; I only know that it's happened."

The comfort Matthew managed to get from holding hands with other people at the end of an AA meeting points to something that seems to be nearly universal for recovering addicts and alcoholics: the relief, the nurturing, the sense of healing that Twelve Step programs can manage to give us has the feeling of being *simple.* Matthew talks about this: "It's like a moment of grace. A sudden flow of acceptance and simplicity, a kind of confluence of feelings—strength, hope, purpose, serenity—all from the touch of a hand. I feel like I've tried to strangle meaning and purpose out of books before this. I was sure that if only my intellect wrestled long and hard enough with the Great Truths of the Universe, it would bring me some kind of answer, some kind of peace. But it's like I was banging against a huge locked steel door for something that was already there, in the air around me. All I had to do was stop for a moment and *breathe.* 'The peace that passeth understanding'—that's a Christian quote, I think, isn't it? Anyway, it comes close to describing what I feel when I manage to let go and let something else besides my intellect take care of me. Healing in recovery happens in the strangest, simplest ways. You don't need a doctorate in philosophy or theology to find it, feel it, benefit from it."

A New Sense of Goals

Matthew is talking about learning a new way to look at and be in the world. No longer is he pursuing "truth" with desperate aggression; sobriety has become for him a way to increase his receptivity to truth, or at least life. As he puts it, "I'm just plain more relaxed now."

Emily, an aspiring singer and dancer, has followed a different route to a similar destination, a route, she says, that "has taught me what I think I'm after isn't always what I really want or need."

Emily's dream from girlhood was to be a performer. "My mother took me to see *A Chorus Line* when I was about nine years old, just after it opened, and I felt from that moment on that I'd found my calling. Since then . . . I'm almost embarrassed to admit all this—I mean, the whole story of *A Chorus Line* is about what so many people hooked on being performers did 'for love'; I know I sound like one big show business cliché. But that's how it started."

Emily begged her mother for dancing lessons and finally convinced her to let her enroll in their small Pennsylvania town's single dance academy. "I had enthusiasm, that's for sure. And maybe some talent. But I also had a lot of baby fat," Emily recalls. "The teacher seemed to think that teaching kids meant discouraging them completely. She was a jewel. 'You'll never amount to anything as a dancer,' she'd tell me. 'You've got almost no talent and you're too fat.' By the time I was thirteen I had developed a nice big dose of self-hatred. I was still overweight, but determined to stick it out at dance classes. By this time I was also singing in my school chorus, and nurturing the idea that if I couldn't become Donna McKechnie in *A Chorus Line*, maybe I could be Barbara Cook. Being overweight didn't stop her from getting accolades as a performer, did it? But to tell the truth, I hated being fat. None of this was helped by my mother, who was and is a svelte, beautiful woman; she'd even modeled before she got married, and she never had a weight problem. I could tell she was humoring me by letting me take dance classes; she never thought her fat little daughter would amount to much either."

But the persistence of Emily's dream of becoming a performer was such that when she was sixteen—and still overweight, and still going to dance class—her mother decided that since no diet had ever worked for her daughter, maybe a prescription for diet pills might help bring Emily's weight down. Emily says this was the turning point of her life. "My mother took me to her doctor, who'd been providing her with diet pills too, to keep her weight down. This guy was a real 'Dr. Feelgood.' A 'give 'em a prescription and get 'em out of the office so I can play golf' kind of guy. Which was fine with me. I loved those pills. They actually did help me to lose weight—a lot of weight. And more than that, they gave me incredible energy. Even the rude teacher at my dance academy began to notice both the weight loss and how fueled-up I suddenly was. 'Maybe I was wrong,' she said. 'Maybe you could make it after all.'"

That was all Emily needed to hear.

The past ten years, she says, have been a maniacal roller-coaster ride. "I did the whole move-to-New York deal. Found a cheap boarding house to live in, took courses at acting studios, private sessions with dance and vocal coaches, all financed by my father, whom I convinced that giving me money for the odd lesson here and there would be cheaper than sending me to college. Who wanted to go to college? I wanted to *perform*—right away! I've had I don't know how many waitress jobs." Emily sighs. "And I've taken I don't know how many pills." Emily had early become convinced that the only way she could make herself even marginally acceptable to anybody, and certainly to anybody who might actually be in the position of getting her an acting job, was to keep rail thin and wildly energetic. "I was convinced I had no resources of my own," she says. "The only thing I could offer was what the pills gave me: an emaciated body and endless nervous energy. And whenever anybody showed the least bit of interest in me, I was *theirs*. Strung out on uppers, I was all but stripping in front of agents: If sex is what it took to get me a job, fine. Or if they wanted to know about some good drug connections, fine too. I was willing to barter anything I was or had for—for what? Attention. That was what I craved all the time. Attention."

For the first four or five years she was in New York, Emily says, "I could at least pretend to be a relatively normal human being. The drugs hadn't made me totally insane yet. I even got this or that job in my field. I was an extra in a few movies; once I got in the chorus for a revival of an old musical, but the funding fell through. Did some off-off-Broadway for free. Formless avant-garde theater—I posed as a refrigerator in one 'play.' I was hardly 'making it,' but I hung on at least to the chance that one day I might."

The drugs seemed eventually to blot out that chance, however. "I was so strung out on uppers that even taking downs didn't seem to calm me down. Some friend on the Lower East Side of Manhattan extolled the virtues of heroin, and soon I was shooting up. That's when it got really bad. I started missing appointments, couldn't even hold on to a waitress job by the end. Went into a crazy screaming fit in the middle of the street, was picked up by the police, who had to handcuff me so that I wouldn't scratch their eyes out, and eventually I ended up in a psychiatric ward." Emily shudders. "You wanna talk low bottoms, boy, that was low. But at least it was a bottom. I knew, after an in-house NA meeting, not only that I was an addict, but that maybe, just maybe, something besides drugs might be out there to help me. It was a revolutionary idea—that I might have a self that existed totally independent of who I was when I was high."

Emily is now nearing the two-year sobriety mark. "The first year I just gave up on my show business dream. It was too tied to drugs, for one thing. But this past year, the itch returned. I managed to help out giving dance classes to junior-high-age kids in an after-school program at the YMCA. I discovered I was actually a pretty good teacher after all my frustrating years of practicing and practicing and getting almost no encouragement, but still learning from practicing. I find that I don't tear people down the way that awful dance teacher back in Pennsylvania tore me down." Emily's new life consists of "yet another waitressing job, but in a fairly upscale coffee shop—good tips and it's not frantic, and now that I'm not strung out all the time, I actually find I can handle it okay. But I've also poured energy into my teaching job at the Y, which pays me almost nothing, but gives me a sense of joy I never experienced from trying to be a performer. Now we stage little plays, dance concerts, we've expanded to some revues from musical shows too—it's really exciting. Somehow in putting my energy into these kids' dreams, into *their* lives, I'm adding meaning to my own.

"About six months ago, though, I went through a really rough period. I'd sprained my ankle getting off a bus—*God*, it was painful. I wound up in the emergency room of a New York hospital right at its peak period: Saturday night. I wasn't seen by anybody for almost four hours, and by that time my ankle had swollen to twice its size. I finally got treated, went home on crutches, and was out of commission for six weeks. I couldn't get in to teach my class, I couldn't work—I had no insurance, no disability, nothing but the kindness of my friends in NA and what little money I'd managed to save. But the financial hardship wasn't the worst part. The worst part was what I did to myself, what my mind spun out for itself during that lone, bleak period. I had a sponsor I called pretty much every day, and once or twice she and some other NA friends all came over and had a meeting in my tiny apartment. That helped. But I still spent most of my time alone, obsessing, projecting, doing a real number on myself. I did a kind of perverse Fourth Step, I suppose. It was an inventory of my life, all right, but all it pointed up was what a terrible failure I'd been. All those years going to dance class, hitting every audition in town, trying desperately to be a success at the one thing I loved—performing—and where was I? An out-of-work waitress who taught kids a few dance steps for next to nothing in a YMCA. Where were the payoffs for all my work, all my dreams? Here I was pushing thirty, and there Madonna was making headlines and doing multimillion-dollar shows, and there was Jodie Foster getting Academy Awards and directing her own films, and there was Michelle Pfeifer being sexy as hell in hit movies, and what was I? A washout. What the hell did sobriety mean, anyway? What real good was it doing me? It hadn't gotten me any closer to my dreams. At least when I took drugs, I had the energy and the nerve to go out there and hit every audition. At least it made me look like a dancer, even if I couldn't get a job as one. Okay, I hadn't gained any weight back yet. Hoo-wee! I'd learned how to keep weight off without diet pills. Aren't I *special?*"

Emily says she descended into a frightening state of cynicism, which gave way to the deepest despair she's known so far in sobriety. "I couldn't call my sponsor in the state I was in. Distantly, I imagined it might be good for me, but I just couldn't bring myself to do it. Luckily, after two or three days of silence on my end, she called me. She must have been pretty alarmed by how I sounded because she said she was coming right over. And she did, bringing a quart of wonderful chicken soup she'd gotten from a kosher delicatessen and a loaf of rye bread. She also brought me my mail, which I hadn't bothered to get for the past few days. And as she busied herself heating up the soup and slicing the bread, I went through the envelopes she'd deposited in my lap. There were a lot of them. A few bills, the usual junk mail. But also six letters addressed to me in childish handwriting. I opened them, one by one, and started to cry. 'Dear Emily, I hate it when you're not here so please come back so that you can teach me how to sing "I Feel Pretty" and dance at the same time the way you said we were going to. By the way, you're the greatest teacher in the world.' 'Dear Emily, Everyone says you'll be back soon but the days go by and you're still not here. Are you in a lot of pain? I hope not. I broke my arm when I was little but it's okay now so don't worry, you'll get better soon. Also, please remember to bring in that pink leotard you said you had for me. I love you.' 'Dear Emily . . .' and four more of the same. Okay, I know it sounds corny. But I was crying. When my sponsor came in with a bowl of soup and she saw me crying, all I could do was point to the cards open all over the bed. She gave me the soup, read the cards, and *she* started to cry too. 'Bunch of sentimental fools we are,' she finally blubbered.

"Something had changed. And it wasn't just my mood. Because after a good long talk with my sponsor and the promise to call her regularly, and to call other friends in the program, after she was long gone and I'd put the cards away, something had lifted in me that, to this day, has stayed lifted. It's hard to explain. But it's like a whole layer of self-hatred isn't in me anymore. For the rest of the time I was laid up, I found I was able to take pleasure in the simple things—I was *allowing* myself to take pleasure in them. Turning on the TV to watch old movies. Eating my chicken soup. Looking out the window at how the light changes from afternoon to evening. I was able to read, to meditate—to somehow *give in* to my own need for healing. I wasn't so afraid anymore. And since then, since I've been able to go back to work and to teaching those kids, it's not like I've given up my dreams, not that I don't still want something better for myself career-wise. I just don't feel the same kind of self-denigrating urgency about it anymore. It's finally beginning to occur to me that I might be able to experience joy and gratitude and peace *right now*, not just at some vague later time when all my dreams of fame and fortune have come true. I've even been able to accept that if they never come true, something I never dreamed of might take their place. That's what happened with this teaching job at the YMCA—it fell into my lap. I don't know what's coming around the corner, ever. But something lifted in me that day with my sponsor and the chicken soup and reading all those cards from my students. I let some love in, some enjoyment. And in an odd way, my goals changed. Or rather, I've since been able to see that maybe there are a number of scenarios that would be just fine in my life. I don't have to be the next Madonna, Jodie Foster, or Michelle Pfeiffer. It might be okay just to be Emily."

Emily also says that she learned a lesson about reaching out: "The seeds I'd planted in NA, going to meetings, developing my friendship with my sponsor and other people in NA, have grown and are starting to bear fruit. God knows how much worse my despair would have been, laid up for six weeks, without the support I got from all that. As it was, I was a basket case. Thank God for whatever it took to get me the help I now know I can depend on."

That help is, Emily says, "for lack of a better word, spiritual as much as anything else. What touches me in my life now, whether it's an expression of support from some program person or from one of my kids in class, is something beyond whatever particular words they say to me. I often think at meetings that it almost wouldn't matter if we just sat there, mumbling incoherently at one another, one after the other—which, come to think of it, is what some meetings can seem like from time to time! It doesn't seem to matter so much what anyone says. It's our *presence* that matters. The fact that we're there, that we're receptive to help, that we're willing to reach out and be available to others reaching out to us. It's the fellowship, I guess, that really heals."

A Spiritual Sense of Self-Acceptance

Emily's new sense of goals in sobriety is a pervasive one, especially in the way her revelation seemed to her to be spiritual. So many people in the second year of recovery go through the kind of disillusionment Emily underwent, the feeling for a long, dark moment that you'll never be what you always dreamed of being, that you're a failure, and that sobriety hasn't helped in the ways you'd hoped it would help. Then, usually through the intervention of someone or something outside yourself, you may experience a kind of illumination, a new light on your life that allows a sense of self-acceptance and gratitude for the strides you *have* made and are continuing to make. This illumination has a quality that can't be quantified as the simple product of, say, using your willpower to better advantage. It isn't, in the experience of recovering people I've talked to, something you're giving yourself on your own. Somehow, whatever insight and relief flood in, they are always greater than the sum of whatever parts triggered them into being. Whatever is going on seems to come from some source outside yourself, some "spiritual" source.

Whatever this spirituality may be, it seems to create a feeling of serenity and simplicity. In fact, taking pleasure in simple things, as Emily realized she could do, becomes a process of healing; the urgency about the fact that you're not some imagined ideal lifts. What you're left with is a wider sense of options, different paths that are open to you. Life isn't as narrow as you once thought it was. Finding this out can't help but be a relief—a relief and a liberation.

David, by his own admission, was in particularly sore need of this kind of liberation. While at first glance his story and the nature of his own illumination may not seem to be especially spiritual, he has come to realize that that's exactly what it was. "If there's one word for me in my second year of sobriety, at least up until about a month ago, it's 'cranky.'" Not that David had always been cranky in sobriety. His story brought him from deep despair to equally strong relief when he was finally able to get sober. But, as you'll see, some things in his life didn't change all that much for him even after he got sober.

"I was a closet drinker; I kept it from everybody. I'd be maniacally busy during the day, working as an accountant, running errands for my mother—my father died ten years ago and my mother has chronic arthritis, so she needs a lot of help with shopping and stuff—then I'd be working on any number of my own little projects, like I've been wanting to write this book for years, and it takes a lot of research at the library—and then, whammo, home every night to big jugs of Italian white wine. I always had a 'good' brand of vino; the fact that I cared what brand of wine I drank was proof to me that I didn't have a drinking problem."

But David's full daily schedule and nightly drinking himself into oblivion finally did him in. "It was years before I realized that maybe it wasn't normal to begin each day by throwing up. It's funny: I washed, brushed my teeth, had a cup of coffee, and threw up. That was my morning ritual. I got so depressed the last few years of my drinking, blaming my lousy life on having to take care of my mother, on never getting any breaks in my career—I'd had the same crummy accounting job for fifteen years, never been promoted, but was too afraid to imagine changing jobs; I was sure I'd never be able to work anywhere else. And my book, which was going to be a huge revisionist look at the world economy, something I envisioned as a text that the general public would also want to read, well, that's what I'd made the center of my dreams. *That's* what was going to make me happy and rich and famous, enable me to make my mark in the world. But I could never get past the research to do any actual writing. My mother, my job, a thousand emergencies in the day, and just plain lousy luck kept getting in my way. Drinking was my 'inspiration' time, I'd always thought, at least until the end."

The end of David's drinking was precipitated by a very strong "power of example": "A guy in my office who'd been thought of as the office drunk, sort of like a town drunk—some offices just seem to need to have one—anyway, he got sober. And the change was incredible. Not only did he look better and treat people more kindly after he stopped drinking, but his productivity just about

tripled. The guy was simply *there* in a way he'd never been before. That's when it occurred to me that maybe my nightly
drinking, which I'd always thought of as inspiration time, the
time I let my imagination soar, when I planned all the wonderful
things that would happen to me after my book got me the
Pulitzer Prize, maybe my drinking was actually *keeping* me from
making my dreams come true, not helping me to attain them. By
this time, I was so depressed and so hung over, so sick, that I was
ready to seriously consider stopping. So I made a lunch date with
this newly sober guy to ask him about what he'd been through,
how he was able to stop. It took some courage for me to do this.
I mean, he'd made no secret about being a lush, and now made
no secret about the fact that he'd stopped drinking. But nobody
knew I had a problem. Hell, nobody knew I *drank!* I never had
anything even at Christmas parties, certainly never at lunch.
But, amazingly, this guy asked no questions. He'd just accepted
that I felt I had a problem, and that night he took me to my first
AA meeting."

It's been about twenty months since David stopped drinking.
"I had a sort of classic experience," he says. " I really was on a
pink cloud just about the whole first year. For one thing, it was
so wonderful to get through the day without throwing up! I just
felt so much better. And while it's never been easy for me to
make friends, even now in AA, I did get a sponsor and have followed his suggestions to make a meeting every day no matter
how I feel. So I feel plugged in, even if there's still this nagging
feeling, sometimes, of being alone. I talk about it, though, and a
lot of people seem to identify when I bring it up, so even that has
become a source of feeling connected. . . ."

David pauses. His expression makes it clear that he hasn't
been pleased with all of what he's experienced in sobriety. "If
anything," he says, "now that I've gotten over the first-year
hump of just proving to myself I can make it, one day at a time,
without resorting to the ol' vino, my life has become more

stuffed with activity—*pointless* activity, it so often seems. It's like I can't get anything completely done. The piles of paper in my house seem about to engulf me. Taking care of my mother has become even more of a burden; the older she gets, the worse her arthritis gets, and the better I get at showing up for her, the more it seems I have to! My job is as much a drag as it ever was, my research on my book goes on endlessly, I always seem to be trying to fit in a trip to the library between going to the store and the library's closing time. I've also started going to this dating workshop for singles over forty. I feel a little embarrassed to admit it, but you know, now that my first year is over and I'm supposed to be able to get into a relationship . . ." David heaves a sad sigh. "But it's like I can't get anything *important* done. Just all these unending, incomplete little bits of things. I feel like my life is running out like the sand in an hourglass. I mean, I'm still sober, and that's great. But my life is far from 'happy, joyous, and free.' Where's the joy that sobriety is supposed to make possible? I feel like a hungry rat in a maze."

In an effort to gain some kind of control over his time and his life, David says he carries around a "To Do"list. At last count, it had thirty-six items on it. "Who'm I kidding? Four hired assistants couldn't get all this stuff done," he says. "I'll tick half of a thing off, maybe one or two other things on the list a day, and make myself crazy with how much stuff remains to be done. I get nuts about this! I can't seem to dig myself out from under it."

Feeling as pressured as he could ever remember feeling, and almost as depressed as he had felt before he stopped drinking, David finally began turning to his sponsor with new energy. "My sponsor's actually younger than I am; he came into the program in his twenties; I was forty-one when I came in. But I've always admired the guy's energy. And I've been jealous of his ability to get things done. So jealous that I almost didn't want to admit to him that I was having the time-scheduling problems I've been having. It seemed like such an admission of weakness. And hell,

I was more than ten years older than he! Wasn't I supposed to know how to organize myself better—wasn't that a part of the territory of growing up? But I kept on hearing about humility in the rooms. It took some courage, but I started to call him more regularly and share how frustrated I was that I couldn't get things done, that I couldn't give my life more meaning."

David's sponsor took a pragmatic tack. "He asked me to actually read him what was on my list of thirty-six items to do. I was embarrassed; I mean, the list was a real motley collection. But I took a deep breath and I read it anyway." David's list included the following:

- Relabel and organize videotapes
- Clean out utility drawer in the kitchen
- Sort through and file six piles of clippings on desk
- See new Scorsese movie
- Volunteer at AIDS clinic
- Look up GNP statistics for my book
- Write my book
- Buy three pairs of black socks
- Ask R for a date
- Pick up Mother's dry cleaning
- Call boss and schedule meeting to ask about raise
- Buy two pots for begonias for living room
- Check to see if there's olive oil in cabinet
- Try out new pesto recipe

. . . and twenty-two other reminders in an equally variegated vein.

"My sponsor let me get to about the twentieth item. Then he stopped me. 'Is there anything on that list you really *want* to do?' he asked me." David pauses, as he did when his sponsor asked him this question. "I was stupefied. It seemed like a ridiculous question. What did my wanting anything have to do with it? It had never occurred to me that that was even important!" But David's sponsor asked him to go through the list again, with this in mind. What did David actually *want* to do?

"It was amazing," David says. "I prefaced everything—even stuff that was supposedly on my list for pleasure, like seeing a movie, trying out a recipe, or asking someone for a date—with 'I have to.' Everything on that list was, to me, a kind of 'must,' something it seemed that somebody *else* was telling me I had to do. There was only one item that didn't seem like a 'must': the research for my book. My sponsor caught the change in tone in my voice. 'Sounds like you enjoy doing that research,' he said. I said, 'Sure, but'—I was quick to push this in—'the *research* isn't the point! It only counts if I turn it into a *book.'*"

When David truly heard what he was saying, helped by his sponsor pointing it out, he realized something crucial, something he'd never allowed himself to realize before. I said at the beginning of David's story that it may not at first seem to illustrate much about "spirituality,"at least as that term is commonly thought of or defined. And yet David said that the nature of his revelation about his "To Do" list was, in fact, an entirely spiritual one. "It's like something let loose in me," he says. "The revelation was simply that I'd never thought that I had the right to do what I wanted to do, and that was a revelation. The spiritual part of it was, for that moment, I felt this flood of *permission*, a feeling of how right and important it was for me to set my priorities according to the dictates of my own heart, of who I really was. It's not that I suddenly got over all my 'musts' and 'shoulds.' But, in the moment, I realized I could look at those supposed imperatives differently. I could question them. Even more amazing, I could legitimately decide not to do them if I concluded that they weren't really important to *me.*

"The general feeling I had of permission seemed to come from someplace else. It was what I've heard in the program is an 'Aha!' moment. Whenever I get an 'Aha!' moment in sobriety, that sudden flood of understanding something not just with my head but in my gut and heart, I feel like I'm aligning my will with my Higher Power's will. I feel like I'm no longer in conflict with 'God.' It's like you struggle and struggle to fit in a certain piece of the jigsaw puzzle and it just won't go—and, suddenly, it seems to find its own slot, fits in beautifully, perfectly: It's arrived. That was the nature of the 'rightness' I felt when my sponsor got me to question what I could see was really the lack of priorities in my life. I'd lacked priorities because I'd lacked trust in myself. Once I allowed that trust to come in, the 'musts' and 'shoulds' of my life reorganized themselves. It became clearer to me what the next right thing to do really was."

One of the things David now realizes and accepts more about himself is that he genuinely likes the process of research. "I'm accepting that I like being a kind of pack rat. I take a real pleasure in playing detective, looking for obscure facts, fitting them together. What I also realize—and this is painful, because it means taking a new look at what I thought I wanted to do—is I *hate* writing. The reason I haven't started writing my book yet is because deep down I really don't want to. The reason I beat myself up for not wanting to is because my ego was so attached to creating a masterpiece; I thought it was somehow *expected* of me to do great things. But now that I'm honest with myself, I see that I just want to kind of dig around in the library and find things out. I'm not sure how much further I want to take it beyond that."

For David, the relief of discovering that it's all right to do what you want to do has been profound. "It's like I'm learning how to let up on myself," he says. "I'm not fighting who I am. And this little seed has already taken root and is starting to grow in other areas of my life. How much do I fight myself every day, doing things I really don't want to but I think are somehow expected of me? Really, when I look at what it took to get me sober, it was that I *wanted* to get sober. That's really why I've been able to let sobriety into my life. I wanted it—simple as that. But what I didn't realize until now is that that same principle works in every other aspect of my life too. I'm allowing myself to follow my heart, just as I allowed myself to follow my heart in getting sober. And the feeling of this is spiritual. I suddenly feel a kind of overwhelming goodwill from the very center of me, which is where I've always felt the presence of a Higher Power. My 'God' isn't somewhere up in the heavens; it's right in my heart. And all I've ever really needed to do was go back there, back into my heart, and listen. Maybe that's the best way I can describe what spirituality means in my life: It's that process of going back down to the center of me, allowing myself to be still, allowing myself to listen."

A Spiritual Sense of Success

The process of experiencing spirituality in sobriety seems to be as varied and individual as each recovering person is. Adele is clear that she "plugs in" to a spiritual sense of recovery pretty much exclusively by attending NA and AA meetings. She says she needs "people around. It's only by reinforcing again and again that I'm not alone, that there are other people going through what I'm going through, that I seem to get better. And that I seem to discover more about the Higher Power with which I'm supposed to be developing all this conscious contact."

Adele, at thirty-five, is the mother of three small boys, four, six, and eight years old, and until recently, felt that the only role open to her was "wife and mother. My husband never drank, thank God, although his mother was alcoholic—one reason I think he was attracted to me! Anyway, he's always been a good provider, and while I was drinking and taking pills, he was also a good enabler. He'd call in his sister or his mother or a neighbor to help with the cleaning and cooking; at one point, my whole neighborhood was taking care of stuff I just couldn't seem to get done myself. I was always 'sick.' 'Oh, Adele is having one of her episodes,' my husband would say, and someone else would come in and make lunch for the kids or bring in a casserole for dinner or help with the wash. I feel some of my greatest shame about not being there for anybody, those last years of my drinking and drugging."

Adele's "episodes" finally got her to go to a therapist. This became the bridge to getting help in a rehab. "It didn't take right off," Adele says. "I found I could give up drinking when I got out of rehab, but I couldn't imagine life without taking my pain pills; I was hooked on Percodan and Valium. It took me several tries before what they were saying at the Twelve Step meetings began to make sense." Now, Adele says "miraculously,"she's coming up on her second anniversary of sobriety in both AA and NA.

"This second year has been amazing,"she says. "For one thing, I've gone back to school. I'm going to college for the first time."Adele's first year of sobriety, like so many other recovering people's, was concentrated almost solely on learning to do the most basic things sober. "I hadn't really taken care of my family—or myself—for so long, that just making us all lunch or dinner was, and sometimes still is, a big production number. It's been hard taking on responsibilities I was just too zonked out to take on before. I've needed a lot of help. I rely heavily on my sponsor, a woman who's got young kids herself. And I'm on the phone, when I can be, to a number of really close friends from my NA and AA meetings. My husband's going to Al-Anon too, which has turned out to be great for both of us, even if it's meant some awkward adjustments. A lot of money is going to baby-sitters, for one thing; meetings for both my husband and me are so crucial. I know I still need a lot more recovery before I can make it up to my kids! But, one day at a time, this great big awkward life of ours seems to inch forward."

Adele's progress in her second year had also been marked by success in her freshman year of college, which she's attending at night and on weekends. "This has been the most incredible boost for me,"she says. "Not that it started out that way. I mean, I signed up for a psychology course, for example, that I was sure I'd ace without batting an eyelash. After all the therapy I'd been through, all the crises in my life, I was sure I could have *taught* a psychology course! But I got a C- on my first paper and flunked my first quiz. I was about to quit right then and there. Except I didn't. It was a challenge, and my ego took a beating, but something in me sort of dug in its heels, and I stayed. I learned to study, something I couldn't have done in my first year of sobriety. Something, in fact, I'd never done in my life. I took notes and read things carefully and asked questions about things I didn't understand. And now I'm near the head of the class!"

But the exhilaration of her success in school has been double-edged. "You don't know how incompetent I've felt my whole life,"Adele says. "In the past, especially when I drank and took drugs, I always threw up my hands at the least crisis. Getting married meant something very simple and basic for me: finding someone who would take care of me. And Harry, my husband, was only too willing to fit that bill, maybe because he's grown up as a caretaker in his own family. Anyway, now that I'm sober, I've started to show up for my kids more, take care of the house more, actually do well in school! It's like this whole new self emerged: This wonderful, unsuspected, competent person suddenly appeared! The feeling of taking control of my life was heady. It was, really, like finding another drug. And that's where the problem is."

Now, Adele says, "successes can't come fast enough. If I haven't made the best apple pie anyone ever made in the history of baking, if I haven't gotten yet another A on a paper or a test, if I don't get an accolade for every effort I make, some part of me is devastated. This is terribly embarrassing for me to admit. But I can't take criticism *at all.* At first, Harry treated me with such kid gloves; he knew I hated criticism and he walked on eggshells trying not to cross me. He'd all but genuflect in front of the pork chops I made him! But now that he's going to Al-Anon, he's learning not to be dishonest about his own feelings, which means that, slowly, he's saying what he likes *and* doesn't like about my behavior. This is as new for him as it is for me. It still seems to take so little to destroy me! That's the hardest thing to admit. As well as I'm doing in school, as much improvement as I've made across the board in my daily life, I've still got this image of myself as a stupid, incompetent little girl who's incapable of taking care of herself. It's what I grew up feeling. I was the original wallflower. A 'poor little thing' whose only hope lay in finding someone to take over her life. I was an only child, a very sheltered and protected only child. I know how I feel is pretty classic. But it gives some idea of why, now, when I feel I'm starting to get better and do things well, I've grabbed on to my success with all fours. I don't dare *not* succeed now, it seems."

As a result, Adele has felt more pressured than she remembers feeling when she drank and drugged. "When I made the decision not to escape life, which is really what choosing to be sober amounts to for me, I left myself open for all sorts of feelings I was too out of it to experience before. But I never thought in a million years that one of the most upsetting feelings I'd have would come from *succeeding*. It's bizarre, but in some ways I'm more terrified now than I ever was before. Now I feel I've got to 'keep up the good work' at all costs. Follow whatever I do with something better. It's a terrible pressure. Sometimes I wish I could just climb back into that dark hole I was in when I drank and drugged. Nothing was expected of me back there. I didn't have to keep *trying* so hard. . . ."

Adele talked about some of these feelings at meetings, but she tended to downplay them. "It seemed like such a luxury problem, to be complaining about succeeding!" But a moment of illumination came for her when she was asked by a friend to speak at a meeting in a different part of town, a meeting she's never gone to before. "I was nervous," Adele says. "I knew the people at my home groups of AA and NA, and felt comfortable being with them, but what would people I didn't know think of me? I tried to think of big high drama things to say, things that would get their sympathy. But my story hadn't really been very dramatic. I mean, I hadn't done anything wild or outrageous, I just kept to my room and drank and drugged myself into oblivion. I had a very small, very uneventful life when I was active. I couldn't imagine how I could entice anyone—how I could entertain them with my story. And to go on and on about my successes at school seemed like bragging! Such an upwelling of self-hate hit me. I'd never turned down a speaking engagement before, but I really felt I wanted to turn down this one."

Adele felt considerably worse when she realized that the new meeting she was to speak at was known for its "hard-core"members: "It was the Salvation Army building, and most of the men and women there were right out of detoxes and rehabs. In and out of sobriety. People with the very hard-core, outrageous, groveling-in-the-mud stories I didn't have. I was really nervous." But she went through with it anyway. "I kept thinking to myself: Keep it simple. Just say what happened, and what it's like now."Adele talked about how lonely and depressed she'd felt growing up. She described what it felt like to lose herself in drinking and drugging, how it was the only relief she'd ever known from her terror of life. She talked about how that relief slowly turned into an even deeper depression as the drugs and alcohol stopped working. And she talked about some of the miracles she's experienced in sobriety: waking up before her kids, making them breakfast, kissing them, telling them she loved them. "I'd rarely been able to see my kids before noon before,"she said. "Now I'm the one who wakes them up."Adele was surprised by how moved *she* was to realize, once again, what her own transformation had been. But none of it prepared her for the response she got from other people at the meeting.

"It was incredible,"she says. "Heroin addicts, real Bowery-type bums, crack addicts, women who'd sold their bodies to get cheap pints of wine—so many people I once thought could never relate to me—they all, every one, told me how much they identified with me. And what pleasure they took in how much time I had in the program! One woman said it was the first time in her life she thought there might be a chance of her making it past one year of sobriety: That was the kind of power of example I was to her. Other people echoed their gratitude for what I'd had to say. There were homeless people, many of them. People in real physical distress. I was reaching them. And they were reaching me."

Adele says she felt a new level of gratitude and spiritual connection from her experience at this meeting. "It was like a heavy, heavy suit of armor fell off me. I started to feel gratitude—instead of terror—not only for the successes I was having in school and in my life but for something far more basic. That I was alive and conscious and able to *give.* That I could feel love for, and express love to, my kids. Somehow the message also came through that it was all right to enjoy what was happening to me—it was all right to enjoy the *miracle* of sobriety.

"It's been a month since I spoke at that meeting."Adele continues. "But there's been a wonderful spillover from it. I've truly been able to let go of my fear of success, which I now see is a deeply ingrained fear of life. I feel I don't have to push myself so hard. My sponsor has a theory about why so many addicts and alcoholics have become such huge, driven successes. They didn't realize they had a choice!"Adele laughs. "I mean, look at how many artists, writers, musicians, and actors have been addicted to drugs or alcohol! Everyone from Tennessee Williams to Jackson Pollock to Marilyn Monroe. Not that we're all geniuses, but we do, most of us, seem to *push* ourselves unmercifully."

The spiritual help Adele now lays claim to has, as she said at the outset, been a direct gift from going to meetings, from "listening to other people talk about their day-to-day lives, from seeing how different people 'practice these principles in all our affairs,' as the Twelfth Step puts it. And the net result for me, at least right now, is feeling that maybe all I have to do is respond to the next cue as consciously and as kindly and as thoughtfully as I can. Maybe I don't have to worry about whether it will get me an A."Adele takes a deep breath. "Maybe I'm on a journey I don't have to *will* myself to complete. Maybe I'm being taken care of after all."

Each of the stories in this book about second-year recoverers, not only in this 'spirituality' section, has been a story about spiritual awakening and awareness. And as you can see, especially in Matthew, Emily, David, and Adele, spiritual help in recovery isn't something that has to come from a church or a temple or a prayer book. Not that religion can't feed or have meaning in sobriety; for people who identify themselves as religious, it often does. But the spirituality my recovering friends (in whatever year of sobriety) tell me about doesn't seem to be dependent on any singular definition of "God"or "Higher Power." We each define it as we need to. And the spirituality we experience on this individual basis seems to have some very practical aspects: It seems to grow, in fact, directly from facing problems encountered in daily life, whether it's getting angry at a checkout person in a supermarket or being devastated by a loved one's illness or death. We have more resources than we realize, so say my recovering friends, to deal with whatever happens in sobriety.

Adele speaks for many people who make it to and past the second-year mark of sobriety. "I'm finding that life is far more buoyant than I thought it was. I'm starting to believe I can recover from anything, even my most frightening feelings. If I let go, I won't fall into some abyss. Something always seems ready to catch me. There's help available to me for whatever I've got to go through. Sure, maybe it's not a pink cloud anymore. And as I open myself to the abundance of life, I also open myself to feeling things on deeper levels, which means pain as well as joy, responsibility as well as freedom. Sobriety doesn't make life easy. What it does is make life *possible."*

That, perhaps, isn't a bad message to take with you into your third year of sobriety.

You've Got to Give It
Away to Keep It

TO:

FROM:

Suggested Reading

The following books are all official "conference-approved" publications of Alcoholics Anonymous, published by AA World Services, Inc., and are available through AA and some bookstores:

Alcoholics Anonymous (The Big Book). 3d ed. New York: Alcoholics Anonymous World Services, Inc., 1976.

Twelve Steps and Twelve Traditions. New York: Alcoholics Anonymous World Services, Inc., 1981.

As Bill Sees It. New York: Alcoholics Anonymous World Services, Inc., 1967.

Living Sober. New York: Alcoholics Anonymous World Services, Inc., 1975.

Came to Believe. New York: Alcoholics Anonymous World Services, Inc., 1973.

In addition, I heartily recommend the following:

B., Hamilton. *Getting Started in AA.* Center City, Minn.: Hazelden, 1995.

————. *Twelve Step Sponsorship: How It Works.* Center City, Minn.: Hazelden, 1996.

B., Mel. *New Wine: The Spiritual Roots of the Twelve Step Miracle.* Center City, Minn.: Hazelden, 1991.

Carnes, Patrick. *A Gentle Path through the Twelve Steps.* Center City, Minn.: Hazelden, 1993.

————. *Out of the Shadows: Understanding Sexual Addiction.* Center City, Minn.: Hazelden, 1992.

————. *Sexual Anorexia: Overcoming Sexual Self-Hatred.* Center City, Minn.: Hazelden, 1997.

Gorski, Terence T. *Passages through Recovery.* Center City, Minn.: Hazelden, 1997.

Kettelhack, Guy. *Easing the Ache: Gay Men Recovering from Compulsive Behavior.* Center City, Minn.: Hazelden, 1998.

Kominars, Sheppard B., and Kathryn D. Kominars. *Accepting Ourselves and Others: A Journey into Recovery from Addictive and Compulsive Behaviors for Gays, Lesbians and Bisexuals.* Center City, Minn.: Hazelden, 1996.

Kurtz, Ernest. *Not-God: A History of Alcoholics Anonymous.* Center City, Minn.: Hazelden, 1991.

Levine, Stephen. *A Gradual Awakening.* New York: Anchor Books, 1989.

Larsen, Earnie. *Stage II Recovery: Life Beyond Addiction.* San Francisco: HarperSanFrancisco, 1985.

————. *Stage II Relationships: Love Beyond Addiction.* San Francisco: HarperSanFrancisco, 1987.

Martin, John. *Blessed Are the Addicts: The Spiritual Side of Alcoholism, Addiction and Recovery.* New York: Villard, 1991.

Narcotics Anonymous. 5th ed. Van Nuys, Calif.: Narcotics Anonymous World Service Office, Inc., 1988.

Schaeffer, Brenda. *Is It Love or Is It Addiction?* Center City, Minn.: Hazelden, 1997.

Z., Phillip. *A Skeptic's Guide to the Twelve Steps.* Center City, Minn.: Hazelden, 1991.

About the Author

Guy Kettelhack is the author or co-author of more than a dozen nonfiction books, including

First-Year Sobriety: When All That Changes Is Everything

Third-Year Sobriety: Finding Out Who You Really Are

Easing the Ache: Gay Men Recovering from Compulsive Behaviors

Sober and Free: Making Your Recovery Work for You

On a Clear Day You Can See Yourself, with Dr. Sonya Friedman

Love Triangles, with Dr. Bonnie Jacobson

Dancing around the Volcano